AF600483

THE CATHOLIC UNIVERSITY OF AMERICA
CANON LAW STUDIES
Number 76

SUSPENSION EX INFORMATA CONSCIENTIA

A DISSERTATION

Submitted to the Faculty of Canon Law of the Catholic University of America in Partial Fulfillment of the Requirements for the Degree of

DOCTOR OF CANON LAW

BY

Rev. Edwin J. Murphy, C.PP.S., J.C.L.,
Priest of the Society of the Precious Blood

THE CATHOLIC UNIVERSITY OF AMERICA
Washington, D. C.
1932

Imprimi Potest:

Ignatius A. Wagner, C.PP.S., Ph.D.,
Provincialis.

Carthagenae, Ohio, die V Maii, 1932.

Nihil Obstat:

Valentinus Schaaf, O.F.M., J.C.D.,
Censor Deputatus.

Washingtonii, D. C., die XII Maii, 1932.

Imprimatur:

✠Michaelis J. Curley, D.D.,
Archiepiscopus Baltimorensis.

Baltimoriae, die XI Maii, 1932.

Printed by
The Paulist Press
New York, N. Y.

TABLE OF CONTENTS

FOREWORD

In presenting this work to the public, the writer is cognizant of the importance of the subject treated. The *Suspension Ex Informata Conscientia* is an ecclesiastical penalty, imposed under extraordinary circumstances. It is an instrument placed in the hands of ecclesiastical superiors to enable them to safeguard the dignity of the priesthood and the good of souls in the presence of untoward conditions. This peculiar remedy is a measure of such delicate proportions that it must be used only with the utmost caution.

Practically nothing in the English language has been written on this subject since the Code. Even in other languages very little has been written. It was only recently that an *ex professo* treatment of the subject appeared for the first itme. In a work published within the last year Father Suarez has treated of this suspension at some length. To render the question easily intelligible to all his fellow-priests, the writer has attempted a detailed study of this extraordinary remedy.

In the first part of the work, he briefly sketches the history of this suspension from its inception in the Council of Trent down to the present time. No claim is made to historical completeness. The purpose of this brief historical sketch is simply to offer a guide for the proper interpretation of the present law.

In the second part, the present law is treated, and an interpretation is given, sufficient to answer present-day needs. Questions interwoven with this subject, but not specifically pertinent, have been omitted, or else only briefly mentioned. A study of the minute and accurate legislation on the suspension *ex informata conscientia* convinces one of the keen legislative and administrative genius of the Church.

The writer wishes to express his sincere gratitude to his Superiors for the opportunity of advanced studies in the field of Canon Law. To the Faculty of the School of Canon Law of the Catholic University of America, he dedicates this work in grateful appreciation of their untiring interest and generous cooperation during the past two years. The writer is appreciative of the services of all those who have in any way assisted him in the preparation of this monograph; in particular he wishes to thank the Rev. Alfred Zanolar, C.PP.S., who kindly assisted in the final preparation of the manuscript for the press.

INTRODUCTION

In the last title of the Fourth Book of the Code, the Church lays down the laws governing the use of the episcopal power to issue extrajudicial suspensions *ex informata conscientia*. After a very definite insistence upon even the more minute formalities of judicial procedure, or even in the exceptional modes of procedure, of the formalities of a summary procedure, one is struck by the sudden contrast in this last title. In order fully to appreciate the significance and importance of this extraordinary procedure, and to understand it in its full meaning, an acquaintance with the origin and more important elements of its history is necessary.

This law, instituted by the great Council of Trent, created a tremendous stir in the Church, and has enjoyed perhaps the most interesting history of any merely ecclesiastical law. It is something so unique, so different from the other laws of the Church, that a study of it is distinctly fascinating.

Catholics and non-Catholics alike throughout the world have marvelled and do marvel at the wonderful organization of the Catholic Church. Perhaps no civilized nation in the world today has been unaffected by the influence of her administrative genius. Being at once the most monarchic, and at the same time the most democratic, government in the world, she has developed an administrative system superior to which none has ever been developed.

More than any other society, the Catholic Church demands the greatest respect for and obedience to those who are in authority, but at the same time she gives the greatest guarantees of justice to every individual member. One of her most characteristic traits is the precision with which the rights and duties of superiors on the one hand, and the rights and duties of inferiors on the other hand, are determined, so that neither the one nor the other can pass with impunity the limits set to their respective spheres of activity.

In her judicial system the Church has been concerned especially to guard the interests of the individual against even the slightest shadow of tyranny. In this field she has to a large extent taken, as the foundation upon which to build, that marvelous system of Roman Procedure, and through centuries of patient study and painstaking trial she has so perfected the Roman Procedure, that it would be adapted to her policy of conservative protection of the common good and authority, and likewise of the rights of the individuals.

In order that an innocent party would always have sufficient means of proving himself innocent when accused of a crime, the Church during her history has devised various modes of criminal procedure. "Five different modes were employed in the middle ages, sometimes singly, sometimes the one as the complement of the other: accusation, denunciation, inquisition, the procedure of notoriety, and the procedure of the synod. The first three were 'canonized' by the Decretals; the other two sprang from jurisprudence." [1]

The most ancient mode of ecclesiastical procedure in criminal affairs is the evangelical denunciation, which is proposed by Christ Himself: "But if thy brother shall offend against thee, go, and rebuke him between thee and him alone. If he shall hear thee, thou shalt gain thy brother. And if he shall not hear, take with thee one or two more; that in the mouth of two or three witnesses every word shall stand. And if he will not hear them: tell the Church. And if he will not hear the Church, let him be to thee as the heathen and the publican." [2] This procedure consists in denouncing the criminal act to a superior who has the right and duty to correct. However, it should be preceded by a private admonition; should the strictly private admonition prove of no avail, as frequently may be the case, then in the presence of "two or three" the admonition should be repeated; it is only when these preliminary admonitions have failed, that the delinquent is to be denounced to the superior, who then corrects or punishes as he deems proper. This procedure, far from being antiquated, is still to be followed because the law of charity prohibits one from prejudicing the reputation of another without due cause or necessity.[3]

[1] Bourret, *Des Sentences ecclésiastiques*, p. 12.

[2] Matth. XVIII, 15-17.

[3] For a more detailed account of the various modes of Procedure, cf. Droste-Messmer, *Canonical Procedure*, p. 28; Fournier, *Les Officialities au Moyen-Age*, p. 235; and especially Smith, *Elements of Ecclesiastical Law*, II, 144-169.

As in the past, so now the Church is vitally concerned to give an accused person ample means of defence; the natural law itself demands that a person be not condemned unless he has been proved guilty. Consequently, it has been the constant rule in the juridical tradition of the Church that no one be condemned or punished unless judged according to the requirements of canonical procedure. A lone exception to this general principle of law is found in the procedure *ex informata conscientia*, an extrajudicial and extraordinary procedure.[4]

[4] "*Die Suspension ex informata conscientia ist die einzige Strafe welche ohne gerichtliches Verfahren verhängt werden kann.*"—Hinschius, *System des Kathol. Kirchenrechts*, V, 609; cf. also Pierantonelli, *Praxis Fori Ecclesiastici*, p. 254; *ASS*, XIX, 564.

PART I

HISTORICAL SURVEY

CHAPTER I

ORIGIN AND NATURE OF THE LAW

Article I—Origin

The extrajudicial mode of procedure, known as the suspension *ex informata conscientia,* is of comparatively late date. Previous to the Council of Trent, no cleric could be punished by his Bishop except after a formal trial, and from the judgment given in a formal trial an ecclesiastic, who felt that justice had not been accorded to him, could appeal the case. However, considering the various needs of the time, and the crying abuses which had crept into the ranks of the clergy the Council of Trent in the fourteenth session enacted a decree intended to enable the Bishop to cleanse the sanctuary from unworthy priests, who had corrupted it, and from unworthy candidates, who, it was feared, would corrupt it.[1] It does seem strange, however, that the Fathers of Trent, realizing the full significance of the decree which they enacted, should choose so inaccurate and profuse a method of expressing themselves. In the first chapter of the Fourteenth Session it is decreed: [2]

> *Cum honestius ac tutius sit subjecto, debitam praepositis obedientiam impendendo in inferiori ministerio deservire, quam cum praepositorum scandalo, graduum altiorum appetere dignitatem, ei, cui ascensus ad sacros ordines a suo praelato ex quacumque causa, etiam ob occultum crimen, quomodolibet, etiam extrajudicialiter, fuerit interdictus, aut qui a suis ordinibus seu gradibus vel dignitatibus ecclesiasticis fuerit suspensus, nulla contra ipsius praelati voluntatem concessa licentia de se promoveri faciendo aut ad priores ordines, gradus, dignitates sive honores restitutio suffragetur.*[3]

[1] Cf. Kober, *Die Suspension,* p. 65.

[2] Conc. Trid. Sess. XIV, de Reform., c. 1.—Mansi, *Sacrorum Conciliorum,* XXXV, 357: cf. also Pelella, *Canones et Decreta Concilii Tridentini,* p. 86.

[3] An English translation is hardly less profuse than the original Latin; however due to the importance of this decree, a translation is given: "Whereas it is more beseeming and safe for one that is subject, by rendering due obedience to those set over him, to serve in an inferior ministry, than, to the scandal of those set over him, to aspire to the dignity of a more exalted degree;

Here the Council of Trent has conceded the Bishops the right first, to prevent the promotion to orders of those whom the Bishop has for any reason whatever, even for an occult crime, and by an extrajudicial procedure, forbidden to ascend to major orders; secondly, to suspend clerics from the orders which they have already received, and with the effect that no appellate court could overrule the decision of the Bishop.

This is the wording of the original legislation on the suspension *ex informata conscientia*. Unprecise and barely intelligible as it is, it was to undergo a very trying history until it reached its present concise form in the Code. The name itself, *ex informata conscientia,* did not, as is evident from the quoted text, originate in the Council of Trent. Neither is it found in the writings of the canonists immediately after the Council, or in the works of those who wrote in the seventeenth century.[4] It seems to have been used for the first time in a decision of the Sacred Congregation of the Council in 1730.[5] Benedict XIV used it in his Constitution, *Ad Militantes,* of March 30, 1742; [6] and Pius VI in his Bull, *Auctorem Fidei,* of August 28, 1794.[7] It has been used by all later canonists, and thus entered into the parlance of canonical language.

Article II—Nature of the Law

The procedure *ex informata conscientia* is an extrajudicial procedure by which the Bishop, acting upon evidence fully satisfactory

to him, unto whom the ascent to sacred orders shall have been interdicted by his own prelate, from whatsoever cause, be it even on account of some secret crime, or in what manner soever, even extra-judicially; and to him who shall have been suspended from his own orders, or ecclesiastical degrees and dignities; no license, conceded against the will of that said prelate, for causing himself to be promoted, nor any restoration to former orders, degrees, dignities and honours, shall be of any avail."—Waterworth, *The Canons and Decrees of the Council of Trent*, p. 112.

[4] Barbosa, Pirhing, Fagnanus, Pignatelli, De Luca and Gongalez refer to this decree of the extrajudicial suspension of the Council of Trent, but do not call it a suspension *ex informata conscientia.*

[5] S. C. C., *Capritana,* 16 dec. 1730—*Fontes,* n. 3368.

[6] *Fontes,* n. 326.

[7] *Bullarii Romani Continuatio,* VI, Pars III, n. 985.

to himself, prohibits a cleric from ascending to higher orders, or suspends him from the use of the orders already received, on account of a crime known to the Bishop. It is called *ex informata conscientia* because it proceeds, as it were, directly from the informed conscience of the Bishop, which is solely responsible for it. It differs from the ordinary judicial sentence in as far as in the latter the judge must institute a trial according to the rules of canonical procedure; hear the witnesses for and against the accused; allow the accused to defend himself. The decision which he renders must be based upon the evidence set forth in the trial itself, *ex allegatis et probatis,* and must be conformable entirely to the testimony which has been given.[8] Now in the decree *ex informata conscientia* all these formalities of procedure are omitted; there is no trial; witnesses need not necessarily be heard; the defendant need have no opportunity to defend himself; guided only by his own judgment the Bishop pronounces the decree *ex informata conscientia.* Needless to say, this judgment of the Bishop must be based upon solid arguments and he must be certain of the crime in question before issuing such a decree. Otherwise all the laws of justice would cry out against so outrageous a procedure. The arguments must be solid enough not only to convince the Bishop of the fact of the crime, but such as will be able to satisfy the Holy See, for as will be shown in a later chapter, a person, upon whom a suspension *ex informata conscientia* has been inflicted, has a right to have recourse to the Holy See. If recourse is had, the Bishop must forward the proofs to the Sacred Congregation, and although the proofs were such as to render the Bishop himself subjectively certain of the matter, if they are not sufficient to convince the Sacred Congregation, the decree of the Bishop will be overruled. Recourse is allowed in order to make sure that no injustice will be perpetrated, and the Holy See has shown itself prompt at all times to guard the rights of inferiors against the slightest injustice. But even though in a particular case, the decree would be just, because the Bishop is certain of the delinquency, nevertheless if he cannot prove this to the

[8] *Judex tenetur sententiare ex actis et probatis, atque non sufficit ejus extrajudicialis scientia vel informatio."*—De Luca, *Theatrum Veritatis et Justitiae,* Tom. VII, Disc. 36, n. 26.

Holy See, the suspension will be overruled because the Church does not wish the Bishop to proceed with the use of so precarious a measure,[9] unless the Holy See itself can be satisfied of the justice of the proceeding.

Article III—Previous Legislation

This first chapter of the Fourteenth Session of the Council of Trent is indeed an innovation [10] in ecclesiastical legislation, and a unique innovation at that. Here for the first time is the Bishop given the power to set aside the ordinary judicial procedure,[11] and condemn a man, defenseless it would almost seem, for an occult crime which could not be proved in a juridical trial. "Before the promulgation of the law of suspension *ex informata conscientia* of Trent, a bishop was perfectly powerless to punish occult crimes. He could only admonish, exhort, rebuke, threaten the culprit with the Divine Anger, and with the Judgment of God; in a word, before the Council of Trent, a bishop was restricted to moral persuasion only, to induce delinquents guilty of occult crimes to mend their ways." [12] The decree of the Council of Trent introduces a law, the nature of which is such to cause surprise. One would expect to find this decree only after the tendencies in this direction had long been present. Ordinarily laws are developed by a gradual process, the tendencies of which are discernible long before the actual enactment of the law. This holds true particularly of laws of vital importance. However, here, instead of being the result of a gradual development

[9] "*Monarchica facultas infligendi suspensiones ex informata conscientia, summa discretione et in quibusdam tantum adiunctis ab episcopis est adhibenda.*"—S. C. C., 6 iun. 1863—*ASS,* V, 21.

[10] The word "innovation" is not used here in the sense that Sarpi and Van Espen used it, meaning a "usurpation" of power. The Church was certainly within her rights in giving this power to the Bishops. It is here called an "innovation" because it is something new in ecclesiastical law.

[11] Cf. Arndt, "Die Suspension Ex Informata Conscientia,"—*AKKR,* 73 (1895), 141.

[12] *Rights of the Clergy Vindicated,* p. 263; cf. also Molitor, *Kanonisches Gerichtsverfahren,* p. 222.

along similar lines, it is, on the contrary, directly opposed to previous legislation on the same matter.[13]

The contrary law is very precisely stated in the Decretals of Gregory IX, where it is decreed that an occult criminal may be admonished that he should not advance to orders, but he may not be hindered from so doing.[14] This law was given by Alexander III, who was one of the leading canonists of his time. Having been asked by the Archbishop of Bruges concerning the case of a cleric, who on account of his secret crimes the Archbishop judged unfit to be promoted to orders, the Pope in a formal reply answered that because the crime in question was occult, the Archbishop could not hinder the man from being advanced to higher orders: "*Verum tamen, quia peccatum occultum est, si promoveri voluerit eum non potes nec debes aliqua ratione prohibere.*"

A similar decision was given by Gregory IX in 1229.[15] Questioned concerning priests and clerics who had been guilty of grievous crimes, such as adultery, perjury, homicide, the Pontiff replied that those who had committed the crimes, with the exception of homicide,[16] could not be impeded from the use of the orders which they

[13] "*Damnari non valet nisi convictus aut sponte confessus.*"—C. 1, C. II, q. 1. Cf. Bourret, *Des Sentences ecclésiastiques*, p. 19: "*La règle constante du droit, en effet, c'est que nulle peine ne doit être portée contre quelqu'un tant qu'il n'a pas été couvaincu judiciarement du délit dont on l'accuse.*"

[14] "*Ex tenore tuarum literrarum accepimus quod N. clericus adeo deliquit quod, si peccatum eius esset publicum, degraderetur ab ordine iam suscepto, et amplius, non posset ad superiores ordines promoveri. Verum, quoniam peccatum ipsius fore occultum dixisti, mandamus, quatenus poenitentiam ei condignam imponas, et suadeas ut, parte poenitentiae peracta, ordine suscepto utatur; quo contentus existens, ad superiores amplius non ascendat. Verum tamen, quia peccatum occultum est, si promoveri voluerit, eum non potes nec debes aliqua ratione prohibere.*"—C. 4, X, *De Temporibus Ordinationum*, I, 11.

[15] The decision of Gregory IX is taken almost verbatim from a previous decision of Clement III. Cf. Gongalez, *Commentaria Decretalium*, Tom. I, in cap. *Ex Tenore*.

[16] "*Notandum: ab eo quod dictum est criminosum occultum non posse impediri ab exercitio Ordinis suscepti, nec prohiberi quominus ascendere possit ad superiores ordines, excipiendum est crimen homicidii, quod etiamsi occultum maneat, irregularitatem inducit, in qua solus S. Pontifex dispensare potest.*"—Pirhing, *Jus Canonicum*, Lib. I, Tit. XI, Sect. I, n. 18.

had already received, nor could they be prohibited from advancing to higher orders, as long as their crimes could not be proved by a judicial process in accord with the law of criminal procedure.[17] He said, however, that should they refuse to repent they should be admonished, under threat of divine judgment, that they were endangering their eternal salvation by continuing to exercise their orders.[18]

In these decretals, therefore, it is evident that the general law of canonical procedure had to be followed before a man could be refused orders, or could be suspended.[19] The Pre-Tridentine law on this may be briefly summarized: (a) All those guilty of notorious crimes were not allowed to be ordained. (b) All those guilty only of occult crimes could continue in their ministry, especially if they had performed the required penance. An exception was made in the case of homicide; those guilty of homicide even though the crime was occult, could not continue in their ministry without a dispensation. (c) Those guilty only of occult crimes could be promoted to orders, even though their crimes were of such a nature that were they public, they would impede the exercise of orders without a grave sin.[20] Besides the crime of homicide, there was another exception to this general rule, namely the crime of heresy.[21]

A very notable exception to this procedure of the Decretals, if such it may be designated, was quite a different law laid down for

17 *"Ratio est, quia occulta delicta publice vindicanda non sunt, ideoque . . . quia actus publicae potestatis vel administrationis, non secundum privatam scientiam Administrantis, vel judicis, sed secundum publicam notitiam exerceri debeat."*—Pirhing, *Jus Canonicum*, Lib. I, Tit. XI, Sect. I, n. 17.

18 *"Quaesitum est de sacerdotibus et aliis clericis, qui, per reatum adulterii, perjurii, homicidii vel falsi testimonii bonum conscientiae perdiderunt. . . . Respondemus, quod si proposita crimina ordine judiciario comprobata vel alias notoria non fuerint, non debent hi (praeter reos homicidii) post poenitentiam, in jam susceptis vel suscipiendis Ordinibus impediri: qui se non poenituerint, monendi sunt, et sub interminatione divini judicii obtestandi, ut in testimonium suae damnationis in susceptis etiam ordinibus non ministrent."*—C. 17, X, *De Temporibus Ordinationum*, I, 11.

19 Cf. Fagnanus, *Commentaria in V Libros Decretalium*, in cap. *Ex Tenore;* and Gongalez, *Commentaria Perpetua Decretalium*, in cap. *Ex Tenore.*

20 Cf. Leurenius, *Forum Ecclesiasticum*, Lib. I Decret., quest. 507.

21 Bouix, *De Judiciis*, II, 316.

Regulars.[22] This is given in the rubric of the fifth chapter of the eleventh title of the first book of the Decretals: "*Religiosus contra prohibitionem praelati sui ordinari non debet.*" The Law emanates from Lucius III. In answer to a question concerning Regulars by the Archbishop of Tours in 1183, the Pope replied that the Regular Prelates could prohibit their subjects from being advanced to higher orders on account of secret crimes:

Ad aures nostras te significante pervenit quod religiosi quidam zelum Dei habentes ad superiores desiderant ordines promoveri, putantes, majus praemium cumulandum, quo in majore gradu positi sublimius officium fuerint exsecuti; sed praelati eorum desideriis contradicunt. Ideoque dixit fraternitas requirendum, an in inferioribus ordinibus constituti juxta beneplacitum suorum praelatorum, quibus promotio displicet, a superioribus debeant abstinere, an valeant praelatis sui renitentibus promoveri. Tuae igitur questioni taliter respondemus, quod honestius et tutius est subjectis debitam praepositis obedientiam impendendo in inferiori ministerio deservire, quam cum praepositorum scandalo graduum appetere dignitatem. Nec est in hac parte subjectorum desiderium confovendum, quoniam esse potest, quod praelati eorum commissa secreta noverint, ex quibus constat eis quod salva conscientia nequeant sublimari, quia non in sublimitate graduum, sed in amplitudine caritatis acquiritur regnum Dei.[23]

Although this law of Lucius III does not very clearly establish itself as an exception to the general law of the Decretals, nevertheless by virtue of legal interpretation it received that meaning, and served as a precedent for the Tridentine law; the Council of Trent established this power, given by Lucius III for religious only,[24] also for the secular clergy.

[22] Cf. Molitor, *Kanonisches Gerichtsverfahren*, p. 224; Kober, *Die Suspension*, p. 67.

[23] C. 5, X, *De Temporibus Ordinationum*, I, 11. The entire law is quoted here in the text because the Council of Trent used this decree almost verbatim in wording its decree concerning the extrajudicial procedure of suspensions *ex informata conscientia*.

[24] Some authors thought this law of Lucius III extended also to secular prelates, but the common opinion holds with Fagnanus that it applied only to religious. Cf. Bouix, *De Judiciis*, II, 317; Gongalez, *Commentaria Perpetua Decretalium*, in cap. *Ad Aures*.

The Lucian decree, as is evident from the text quoted, is concerned only with what is treated in the first part of the Tridentine measure, namely the prohibition to ascend to higher orders on account of an occult crime. Pallottini goes to great lengths to show that this was also the practice of the early Church.[25] He points out that even in Apostolic times the advancement to orders was to be decided by the Bishop,[26] and this was left entirely to his judgment. This ancient discipline was relaxed in the case of the secular clergy by the Decretals, while it was upheld for religious by Pope Lucius III. Other authors [27] likewise state that the Tridentine measure is in some ways a return to the ancient discipline of the Church,[28] which allowed public penances to be imposed for occult crimes.

In spite of this seeming return to the ancient discipline, it must be admitted that the Tridentine decree did go contrary to the juridical traditions which had been developed throughout the preceding centuries. "Prior to the Council of Trent no ecclesiastic could be punished by his bishop,—v. g., suspended from the exercise of higher orders,—save upon a regular or formal criminal trial, as prescribed by the sacred canons. Hence no occult crime, in the proper sense of the word,—that is, no crime which was not provable,—could be, properly speaking, punished, no matter how enormous it was; for the simple reason that the fact of its being occult precluded the pos-

[25] *Pugna Juris Pontificii Statuentis Suspensiones,* pp. 74-76.

[26] It is well to note here that although this thesis is primarily interested in the decrees of suspension, and not in the decrees prohibiting the advance to orders, frequent reference must be made to the latter also, because the two are closely connected in the historical development of this legislation, and both are comprehended under the general appellation of suspensions *ex informata conscientia.* However, according to the present law, they are not connected. The suspension is treated in canons 2186 to 2194, while the extrajudicial procedure in prohibiting the advance to the reception of orders is given in canons 970 and 2222, §2.

[27] Cf. Lega, *De Judiciis Ecclesiasticis,* IV, n. 386; Lombardi, *Juris Canonici Privati,* III, 387.

[28] *"Es ist in der That nur ein Zurückgehen auf die Principien des Kanonischen Rechtes und auf die apostolische Würde."*—Molitor, *Kanonisches Gerichtsverfahren,* p. 221.

sibility of its being proved juridically, or by such juridical proofs as are required for conviction in a formal canonical trial." [29]

[29] Smith, *Elements of Ecclesiastical Law,* II, n. 1279. Cf. also: *"Nullum enim crimen enorme et depositione dignum dum manet occultum facit irregularem."*—Barbosa, *Collectanea in Jus Pontificium Universum,* in cap. *Ex Tenore.*

CHAPTER II

ACCEPTANCE OF THE LAW

Article I—Motives of the Law

To understand fully the motivating influence which determined the Council of Trent to lay down such a measure, which, at first sight, seems so drastic, cognizance must be taken of the circumstances in which the Catholic Church found itself in the sixteenth century. Surrounded on all sides by religious turmoil and revolution, the Church was perhaps in the midst of the darkest days of her history. Scandals among the clergy, both high and low, had lessened their influence with the faithful, and desolation seemed to have shadowed the fair face of Europe. The gates of hell seemed for the moment to be opening up to crush that which was impregnable; human passions, more akin to diabolical, were unfettered and licentiousness, like the proverbial weed, seemed to spread everywhere. Monastic life, through wealth and luxury, waned; discipline, which thrives on the spirit of the law, yielded to a pharasaical insistence on the external letter of the law, without taking cognizance of the spirit which motivated the law; and more terrible than anything else, sacerdotal zeal seemed to be a thing of the past.[1]

The Council of Trent, considering these terrible conditions for which a remedy had to be found, realized how hopelessly the previous measures by which unworthy candidates were to be kept out of the sanctuary, or by which those already among the elect of the Lord could be punished after they had proved their unworthiness of their high calling, failed in achieving their purpose.[2] Avidly seek-

[1] "*On vit alors un spectacle inouï, un déchaînement de toutes les passions, la lutte de l'insubordination contre le pouvoir, de la tyrannie contre la liberté, de la luxure contre la sainteté du marriage, du sacrilège contre les barrières du cloître et le parvis du sanctuaire.*"—Parayre, *La Sacrée Congrégation du Concile*, liv. I, chap. 1. Cf. Bourret, *Des Sentences Ecclésiastiques*, p. 24.

[2] "*Würde hier der kirchliche Vorgesetzte an die strengen formen des gerichtslichen Verfahrens gebunden sein, so müsste er den Schuldigen un-*

ing pleasure and wealth, and seeing the large possessions in the hands of the Church and the ecclesiastical honors, surpassing in some manner even those of a civil nature, men rushed to the sanctuary, with never a thought of the necessity of being called by God to so high a dignity.[3] To prevent such candidates from being ordained, the bishops found themselves hampered by the inefficacy of the existing legal procedure:

> Each rejection from orders had to be founded on canonical reasons, judicially proved. No crime could be punished until after a canonical trial in which the delinquent had been legally convicted, according to the laws of criminal proceedings. Hence, many unworthy candidates were promoted to Holy Orders, and many crimes remained unpunished, simply because they could not be proved before the tribunal of the law. Bishops had to witness in silence the blamable conduct of clerics who dishonored the sanctuary, because the nature of the guilt escaped legal and judicial proof. Even when the crimes could be sufficiently proved in ecclesiastical court, the accused, by dilatory measures of all kinds, by appeals, by inhibitions extorted from the judges of the court of appeal, might succeed in escaping the deserved punishment, or have it deferred indefinitely, while in the meantime they continued to inflict the faithful by their scandals, and caused the ruin instead of the salvation of souls.[4]

It is not surprising that the Council of Trent found itself impelled to issue such a measure; it is supremely important for the Church to have good priests; even in the old Law priests were supposed to be eminent for their piety and sanctity.[5] In the New Testament there is frequent mention of the sanctity which should be the lot of those who minister to the Lord. St. Paul says that the priests must show themselves in all things as the ministers of God; they must excel for their chastity, their knowledge, their charity, and

gestört im Amte belassen, die Gefahr für das Seelenheil der Gläubigen, das gegebene Aergerniss bliebe bestehen, die Ehre des kirchlichen Dienstes, die Würde und das Ansehen der Disciplin müssten auf die empfindlichste Weise beeinträchtigt werden."—Kober, *Die Suspension*, p. 65.

[3] Cf. Bourret, *Des Sentences Ecclésiastiques*, p. 26.

[4] Stremler, *Des Peines et censures ecclésiastiques*, pp. 310-311; cf. Peries, "Suspension Ex Informata Conscientia,"—*ER*, XV (1896), 3.

[5] "*Sancti estote, quia et ego sanctus sum.*"—Lev., XIX, 2.

their truthfulness.[6] But some of the priests of the sixteenth century did not answer to these requirements; many unworthy men had been advanced to Holy Orders, and had scandalized the faithful and brought shame upon their sacred calling. To prevent such mistakes in the future there was need for a preventive measure, and to correct the mistakes already existing in the priesthood, there was a crying need for a repressive measure. In answer to these needs, the Council of Trent combined a repressive and a preventive measure in the first chapter of the fourteenth session by giving the Bishops this twofold power to proceed extrajudicially.

The salvation of souls has ever been considered as the first law of the Church, and although the rights of some individuals may seem to have been violated by this rather stringent decree, it must be remembered that there are times when the individual must cede his right rather than witness the ruin of souls, and such a time was present at the time of the Council of Trent. The assembled Fathers there realized the tremendous import of their law, but they deemed it necessary to secure the flock entrusted to their care from the attacks of ravening wolves, who disguised their diabolical intent beneath the sacred robes of the priesthood. "It is true that in providing new and stringent measures for this purpose, it might happen that some innocent persons would suffer, while cunning or flattering culprits turned aside the bolt that should fall upon them." [7] However, in general, the purpose intended by the Tridentine Fathers—the restoration of the honor of the Church and the dignity of the clerical state which had been sullied by unworthy ministers, and particularly the protection of the faithful in their faith and morals against those who were appointed paradoxically to be their shepherds—has been accomplished. Occasionally an ecclesiastical superior, too much concerned with the exercise of his own authority, has been almost tyrannical in abusing this power; however, the history of the last three centuries shows that generally this power has

[6] "But in all things let us exhibit ourselves as the ministers of God, in much patience, . . . in chastity, in knowledge, in long-suffering, in sweetness, in the Holy Ghost, in charity unfeigned, in the word of truth, in the power of God; by the armor of justice on the right hand and on the left . . ."—I Cor., VI, 4-6.

[7] Perics, "Suspensicn ex Informata Conscientia,"—*ER*, XV (1896), 3.

been exercised with prudence and justice, and the beneficial results of this wise legislation have been manifest in the restoration of the clergy to its pristine virtue and nobility, so that its dignity is now universally respected.[8]

Article II—Reaction to the Law

That this law of the Council of Trent created a profound stir in the Church is not surprising when one considers the extreme conservatism of the Church. Her institutions and laws have been perfected and attuned to meet the slowly changing needs of the time. Now after so perfectly developing her judicial procedure through centuries of experimentation, after establishing a juridical tradition, the principles of which were deemed unapproachable and almost unchangeable, a radical change is introduced into her system, and a notable exception is made to her ordinary procedure. Naturally one would expect to find quite a reaction against so sudden a change, and among even her most loyal sons, a sort of hesitant fear was felt in the face of this unexpected discipline. Then also the language of the Council of Trent was so unclear as to leave a doubt in the minds of many as to just what was meant by this legislation. It was only after this law was thoroughly discussed by canonical writers, and repeated decisions had been given by the Holy See, that its exact meaning became known, and men began to realize just what was legislated.[9]

This decree necessarily underwent the same fire of attack, to which all the salutary dispositions of the Council of Trent were subjected. Heresy, impiety, and licentiousness strove with the force of a dying creature to keep the hearts of the faithful grasped in

[8] *"Que de vices ce droit bien appliqué a extirpés de L'Eglise! Que de candidats indignes il a écartés des Ordres! Que de mauvais clercs ont été arrêtés sur la pente du libertinage ou chassés des rangs de l'armée qu'ils trahissaient! Incontinence et Simonie, luxe éhonté et moeurs sybaritiques, plaies hideuses qui expliquent sans la justifier l'hérésie protestante, si tous ces maux ont disparu de l'Eglise depuis trois siècles, c'est aux hommes qui votèrent le décret sur les sentences ex informata conscientia qu'en revient le mérite. L'histoire leur doit ce témoignage!"*—Bourret, *Des Sentences ecclésiastiques*, p. 27.

[9] Cf. Molitor, *Kanonisches Gerichtsverfahren*, p. 224.

their icy hand; from within and without the Church's efforts were hindered at every move, and the return to her former state of purity of morals and faith was accomplished only with the most persistent efforts. History records the outrages and the blasphemies to which these decrees were subjected.[10] A peculiar prejudice against the reformatory decrees prevailed among lawyers and politicians. The civil governments strove against those who would protect and defend the powers of the Pope and Bishops, who would uphold the ancient teaching on the authority of the members of the ruling body in the Church. An attempt to subjugate the Church to the whims of the civil power was continued through the centuries.[11]

Besides this general opposition to the decrees of the Council of Trent, the decree concerning the extrajudicial procedure was the target for many special attacks. The Jansenists and the Gallicans, especially Van Espen [12] and Gibert [13] were the most relentless adversaries of this law. Defeated in all their other arguments they took advantage of the rather obscure reading of the text of the decree, and intent upon weakening as far as possible the external power of the Church, they tried to limit the force of the decree for the procedure *ex informata conscientia,* letting it apply only to the power to prohibit the ascent to orders, but not to suspend.[14] The Bishops, they argue, have the power to prevent a candidate from entering sacred orders, even for an occult crime, but he has not the power to suspend for the same reason, and by extrajudicial proce-

[10] Cf. Bourret, *Des Sentences,* p. 26.

[11] The main purpose of Pallottini in his *Pugna Juris Pontificii Statuentis Suspensiones* was to defend the Tridentine decree *ex informata conscientia* against the attacks of the civil powers; he very ably refutes every objection which they bring against it, and demonstrates conclusively the right of the Church to be unhampered in her disciplinary laws by the *Placet* of kings or emperors; he shows that despite all the opposition the Church will emerge triumphant from every attack.

[12] *Jus Ecclesiasticum Universum,* Part II, sect. 1, tit. X, cap. VI.

[13] *Corporis Juris Prologomena,* Part I, tit. XXII; cf. S. C. C., *Lucionen.,* 8 apr. 1848—*ASS,* XIV, 299.

[14] Cf. Hinschius, *System des Kathol. Kirchenrechts,* V. 609; Kober, *Die Suspension,* p. 68; Molitor, *Kanonisches Gerichtsverfahren,* p. 224.

dure those already ordained.[15] The words *ex quacumque causa, etiam ob occultum crimen, quomodolibet, etiam extrajudicialiter,* are found only in the first part of the phrase, and the opponents refused absolutely to allow their extension to the second part of the phrase, relative to suspensions. The legal developments which arose from this question lasted over a century and form one of the most interesting chapters in the legislative history of the Church. In the following article the most salient features of this development will be given briefly.

Article III—Vindication and Interpretation

Already in the seventeenth century Fagnanus, without being able to understand the seeming ambiguity of the Tridentine phraseology, refuted the objection which was later raised by the enemies of this decree.[16] Although the words, *ex quacumque causa,* etc., are expressed only in the first part of the decree, where there is question of the prohibition to approach orders, they must nevertheless be considered as repeated in the second part which deals with suspension: because the Council, while speaking in one and the same phrase of suspension and the reception of orders, wishes consequently to rule equally on these cases; then likewise, if the contrary be true, the Council in the second part of the decree would be conferring no power on the bishops. Nobody can doubt that the Bishops already had the power to suspend a priest for a public crime by means of judicial procedure.[17]

The force of Fagnanus' argumentation, particularly of his second argument is substantiated by a study of the preamble to this

[15] "*Episcopum posse in vim decreti Conc. Trid., Sess. XIV, cap. 1, de Reform., suspendere clericum ab ordinibus susceptis . . . ob occultum crimen ipso Praelato notum, idque etiam extrajudicialiter, nec Decreto Concilii, nec sanctis canonibus conforme est.*"—Van Espen, *Jus Ecclesiasticum Universum,* Part II, Sect. 1, tit. X, cap. VI, n. 28.

[16] *Commentarium in V Libros Decretalium, in cap. Ad Aures,* Lib. 1, n. 7; similar arguments are advanced by Gongalez, *Commentaria Perpetua Decretalium,* in cap. *Ex Tenore;* Benedict XIV, *De Synodo Dioecesana,* Lib. 12, c. 8; Ferraris, *Bibliotheca,* verbo *Suspensio,* art. 1.

[17] Cf. Bouix, *De Judiciis,* II, 309; Molitor, *Kanonisches Gerichtsverfahren,* p. 224; Kober, *Die Suspension,* p. 68.

decree.[18] To understand the full meaning of a decree, one naturally looks to the preamble to see what purpose was influencing the legislator, or to determine the mind of the legislator. A study of the preamble to this particular decree throws a very interesting light on the argument in question:

> *Cum proprie episcoporum munus sit subditorum omnium vitia redarguere, hoc illis praecipue cavendum erit, ne clerici, praesertim ad animarum curam constituti, criminosi sint, neve inhonestam vitam ipsis conniventibus ducant. Nam si eos pravis et corruptis moribus esse permittunt, quo pacto laicos de ipsorum vitiis redarguent, qui uno ab eis sermone convinci possent, quod clericos ipsis patiantur esse deteriores? Qua etiam libertate laicos corripere poterunt sacerdotes, cum tacita sibi ipsi respondeant, eadem se admisisse quae corripiunt? . . . Ut autem ipsi episcopi id liberius exequi, ac quoquam praetextu desuper, impediri nequeant, eadem sacrosancta oecumenica et generalis Synodus Tridentina, praesentibus in ea eisdem Apostolicae Sedis legato et nunciis, hos qui sequuntur canones statuendos et decernendos duxit.*[19]

The Council, after establishing from Scripture and reason, the necessity of sanctity in the clergy and the duty of the Bishop to see to it that the priests under his authority live worthy of their sacred vocation, deems it necessary to give to the Bishops such means as will be efficacious in remedying the evil. In view of these reasons, therefore the Sacred Synod, in virtue of its sovereign power, decrees the following canons, and the first of these is the decree concerning the suspension *ex informata conscientia*. After such a preamble, is it reasonable to suppose that the Council would then give no power to the Bishops, except that which they possessed already, and which in the past had proved inefficacious to remedy the evils existing in the ranks of the clergy? [20] The arguments of the opponents, restricting the extrajudicial power of this decree to the promotion to orders, are not to the point, since the preamble of the decree says nothing whatever about the promotion to orders, but is interested in eradicating the scandals existing in the clergy already ordained.

[18] Cf. Molitor, *Kanonisches Gerichtsverfahren*, p. 224.

[19] Conc. Trid., Sess. XIV, *de Reform.*, cap. 1, *Prooemium*.

[20] Kober, *Die Suspension*, p. 68.

Although the Jansenists and Gallicans were intentionally trying to insist upon undue restrictions in the interpretation of this law, the Catholic writers themselves were not so certain as to the precise extension of the law. Through a long series, therefore, of authentic interpretations, this obscurely-worded law was gradually understood in the light in which it was issued. In reply to repeated questions the Sacred Congregation of the Council, which was instituted to interpret the decrees of the Council of Trent, has affirmed the character, the extension, and the precise meaning of this decree. Regarding the main point of contention, the words *etiam ob occultum crimen etiam extrajudicialiter,* the Congregation has frequently affirmed that they apply to both parts of the decree, the prohibition to orders, and the suspension from orders. Replies given in 1593,[21] 1623,[22] and 1643[23] implicitly settled this point. It was explicitly answered in 1657. The question was proposed on Nov. 10, 1657, but not being settled immediately, was again proposed by the Bishop of Aleria in the following week. He asked whether the words *ob occultum crimen, quomodolibet etiam extrajudicialiter,* which are expressed only in the first part of the phrase, are to be considered as repeated in the second part. In other words, he asked whether the Bishop had the power to prohibit only the approach to orders for an occult crime, and extrajudicially, or whether he could likewise suspend one from orders for an occult crime and extrajudicially. The Sacred Congregation, after giving due deliberation to the question, replied on Nov. 24, 1657, that there was no reason to recede from the ancient decisions which had been given to the repeated proposal of this doubt, and consequently replied affirmatively.[24]

In 1654 after the Vicar General of Bologna had asked whether the Ordinaries of places could, in virtue of the power given them by the Council of Trent, suspended, for legitimate cause, also extrajudicially, clerics and secular priests, even pastors subject to them, so

[21] S. C. C., *Nullius,* 3 feb. 1593—*Fontes,* n. 2254.

[22] S. C. C., *Sagonen.,* 21 iun. 1623—*Fontes,* n. 2442. It is interesting to note that Benedict XIV, *De Synodo Dioecesana,* Lib. XII, cap. 8, n. 5, misquotes this date assigning it to 1625, and that numerous authors copied his mistake.

[23] S. C. C., *Vercellen.,* 21 mart. 1643—*Fontes,* n. 2642.

[24] S. C. C., *Alerien.,* 24 nov. 1657,—*Fontes,* n. 2752.

that the suspended clerics would not have the right of appeal, the Sacred Congregation replied that Ordinaries did have this power.[25]

In 1730 a similar reply from the Holy See was to the same effect. The Bishop of Capra had suspended *ex informata conscientia* two priests from saying Mass. By an appeal to the metropolitan they succeeded in obtaining an inhibitory decree against their Bishop. The case was fought back and forth, and finally the Bishop appealed to the Sacred Congregation and the suspension *ex informata conscientia* was upheld.[26]

In spite of these repeated decisions of the Sacred Congregation that the Bishops did have the power to suspend their subjects for occult crimes, even extrajudicially, in virtue of the first chapter of the Fourteenth Session of the Council of Trent, numerous protestations were made against the use of this power. It was necessary therefore for the Supreme Pontiff to declare in a pontifical document that the refusal to recognize this power in the Bishops constituted a true rebellion against the authority of the Church. In his Bull, condemning the Synod of Pistoia, he branded as false, dangerous and injurious to the Council of Trent, the proposition which condemns as null and void the suspensions *ex informata conscientia;* he says it was an insult to the jurisdiction of the Prelates of the Church to hold that the Bishops could not use the power to suspend *ex informata conscientia,* which had been given them by the Council of Trent.[27]

The episcopal power to proceed extrajudicially in suspending from the exercise of orders, has been repeatedly confirmed by later decisions and pronouncements of the Holy See. In its instruction of June 11, 1880, the Sacred Congregation of Bishops and Regulars says:

[25] S. C. C., *Bononien.,* 14 nov. 1654,—*Fontes,* n. 2741.

[26] S. C. C., *Capritan.,* 16 dec. 1730—*Fontes,* n. 3368. A similar decision was rendered in 1735 when the Bishop of Tarente asked concerning the case of John Donatus. Cf. S. C. C., *Tarentina,* 20 aug., 24 sept. 1735—*Fontes,* n. 3445, 3447. Cf. also S. C. C., *Iserien.,* 20 dec. 1687—Pallottini, *Collectio . . . S. Congregationis S. C. Tridentini,* sub verbo *suspensio,* XVI, n. 135.

[27] Pius VI, Const. *Auctorem Fidei,* 28 aug. 1794, prop. 49, 50—*Bullarii Romani Continuatio,* VI, Pars III, n. 985.

Plenam quoque vim servat suam extrajudiciale remedium ex informata conscientia pro criminibus occultis, quod decrevit s. Trident. Synodus in Sess. XIV, cap. 1, de reform., adhibendum cum illis regulis et reservationibus, quas constanter servavit pro dicti capitis interpretatione S. C. Congregatio in pluribus resolutionibus et praecipue in Bosnien. et Sirmien., 20 Dec. 1873.[28]

In its Instruction of Oct. 20, 1884, the Sacred Congregation of the Propagation of the Faith further confirmed the right of the Bishop to the exercise of this power. The instruction refers to this law of the Council of Trent as being instituted *sapientissimo consilio.*[29] Finally the Code very definitely includes the suspension *ex informata conscientia* in the general legislation for the whole Church.

After the Papal Constitution *Auctorem Fidei,* controversy was at an end concerning the right of the Bishop to use this power. However, even after that, canonists still varied somewhat in their interpretation or rather in their explanation of the application of the phrase *ex quacumque causa etiam ob occultum crimen,* etc., to each part of the Tridentine Decree. Pierantonelli, in explaining this passage, maintains that, although the words apply to both members of the decree, still they apply to a different extent.[30] This is a consequence of that well-known adage, *Turpius ejicitur quam non admittitur hospes.* In the first case there is a refusal of a right not yet acquired; while in the second a *jus quaesitum* is taken away. Therefore the prelate should not have the same liberty of action in both cases. A cause, even without guilt, may suffice for the Bishop to refuse ordination, if he judges it necessary for safeguarding the dignity of the ecclesiastical state, or for the utility of his diocese. But the motive which can induce him to prohibit the exercise of orders already received, must partake of the nature of a true crime.[31] In other words, this author argues that the Bishop needs a graver reason to inflict a suspension than to forbid an ordination, because

[28] Art. 9—*Fontes,* n. 2005.

[29] *ASS,* XIX, 561.

[30] *Praxis Fori Ecclesiastici,* p. 242.

[31] It will be shown in a later chapter that the only cause for a suspension *ex informata conscientia* is a crime. Other cases are taken care of according to the general norms of the Code.

the penalty inflicted in the former case is graver than in the latter case.[32]

Although the power of the Bishops to proceed extrajudicially has no longer been attacked by Catholic writers after the constitution *Auctorem Fidei,* this does not mean however that it has been popular. Quite the reverse is true. Authors seeking for a reason for its unpopularity have held various opinions; Muniz ascribes it to an ignorance of the real meaning of the law.[33] The absence in this extraordinary measure of the usual formalities of judicial procedure lays it open to the danger of abuse. That abuses have occurred nobody will deny. However it would be rash to overlook its usefulness and view only the abuses that have crept in; still this seems to have been the attitude taken by some. Claiming that it is contrary to the most fundamental principles of the natural law in depriving the accused of the right to self-defense, since he is not necessarily invited to present himself before his judge, and since officially he is punished for something of which he is ignorant, because the Bishop has no obligation to reveal the cause of the suspension, they say it is a tyrannical measure which should be repudiated by an enlightened culture. The influence of Van Espen and other Gallicans is discernible in such an attitude. With Muniz it can be said that a little enlightenment would suffice to prove the falsity of such an attitude. If this episcopal suspension were perpetual,[34] and if there existed no means of control over this procedure, then indeed it would lay itself open to the charge of violating one of the most treasured possessions of man, the right of the individual to justice. But this is not the case; the suspension is of a temporary character, and the minuteness of its discipline is outlined to prevent it from becoming an abuse; any person against whom a suspension *ex informata conscientia* has been issued has the right to have recourse to the Holy See, and the history of the decisions of the Holy See on this question

[32] Cf. also Wernz-Vidal, *Jus Canonicum,* VI, n. 794.

[33] *Procedimientos Eclesiasticos,* I, n. 707.

[34] It is curious to note that in a decision in 1593, the Sacred Congregation held that it could be perpetual,—S. C. C., *Nullius,* 3 feb. 1593—*Fontes,* n. 2254. However in many later decisions perpetual suspensions have not been upheld. The time element of the suspension is treated in a later chapter.

prove amply that the rights of individuals are respected and, when it is found that Bishops had violated these rights, their suspensions were declared null and void, and they were commanded to make reparation of the damages to the injured party.

The Church in making use of this extrajudicial procedure is but making use of the natural rights of a perfect society to insure the accomplishment of her welfare in the face of opposition. This extrajudicial procedure is not limited to ecclesiastical government. Every state finds itself at times impelled to make use of a similar procedure. The repressive measures used by governments against public gatherings of a seditious character is but one example of the civil application of extrajudicial procedure.

Far from being an abuse, contrary to the natural law, this extrajudicial power of the Bishops is a very useful instrument in the hands of the Bishop to insure the good government of his diocese. Cavagnis very ably points out its utility and necessity:

> Since the purpose of the ecclesiastical ministry is the good of the Church, it is evident that it may be useful that certain unworthy persons be repelled from this ministry extrajudicially, not only by forbidding them to enter it, but also by the interdict of the exercise of the functions in it. Sometimes this is a very useful and even necessary measure. Since the Bishop can use this faculty only by way of exception, and since it is provisory, because of the possible recourse to the Holy See, although some inconveniences may result from it, nevertheless the power *ex informata conscientia* should be tolerated on account of the public spiritual good. . . . Without it good government would sometimes be impossible.[35]

Before the Code, some authors went so far as to clamor for its abolition. They argued that the extrajudicial procedure was an improvised means of dealing with the situation existing in the sixteenth century and its use was no longer practicable today. However the fallacy of their reasoning is evident. Although perhaps not so vitally or frequently necessary today as it was then, still the benefits resulting from its prudent use are sufficient to entitle it to a permanent place in the legislation of the Church. Bouix maintains that the question as to the advisability of doing away with this power is open

[35] *Institutiones Juris Publici,* II, 44.

to discussion and that a Catholic may hold either opinion.[36] Smith says:

> That our times are no longer the same as those when the Council of Trent enacted the decree in question, seems beyond doubt. The moral depravity among no small number of the clergy in the days of the Council of Trent certainly warranted such an extreme remedy as the power conferred on Bishops in its XIV Session, chapter 1, de ref. At the present day this reason cannot be said to exist any longer.[37]

This argument may look rather plausible at first sight. It can not be doubted that the standard of the clergy today is much higher than in the sixteenth century; however, in order to maintain it at such a high level, an extrajudicial procedure will often prove useful and even necessary, as Cavagnis pointed out in the words quoted above. And after all, it seems but reasonable to acknowledge that the Church, in view of her long experience in dealing with human nature at all times and in all climes, is the best judge of the opportuness of this extrajudicial procedure. That she has retained it in the Code is sufficient to show her attitude on this question.

Another argument advanced by Smith is:

> The unfavorable impression which is created among non-Catholic even by an appearance of an arbitrary procedure on the part of ecclesiastical prelates would certainly make it advisable for superiors to make use of this power rarely.[38]

Why the use of a power which is clearly within the rights of the Church, and which has been demonstrated to be of such vital importance in preserving ecclesiastical discipline, should be abolished because it creates an unfavorable impression among those who do not know even its nature or purpose, is beyond comprehension. Surely should any one wish to offer rational objections to it, he should first be thoroughly acquainted with it. And anyone familiar with the nature of the power, with the very detailed conditions under which it can be exercised, must certainly admit that it is not a merely arbi-

[36] *De Judiciis,* II, 364.

[37] *Elements of Ecclesiastical Law,* II, n. 1284.

[38] *Elements of Ecclesiastical Law,* II, n. 1284.

trary procedure. If abused, the power to proceed *ex informata conscientia* would indeed be a terrible instrument of tyrannical oppression. That it can be abused is equally evident. But a measure is not to be judged from its occasional abuse but rather from its use. The history of the last three centuries have shown the Holy See very prompt to check every abuse in this matter.

Pierantonelli justly remarks that those who would cry out on finding a scandal among the clergy, bitterly attack the Bishops if they employ the remedy placed at their disposal by the Church to cure the infirmities of the clergy.[39] It must be borne in mind that the graces of Holy Orders, although great and powerful, do not take away from a priest his human nature with all its tendencies to evil. Circumstances may arise in which the priest, buffeted by many and grave temptations, may neglect the means of grace at his disposal and thus succumb to the weakness of his nature. "He has not yet scandalized the faithful; but he has been weak, and the watchful eye of the bishop, fixed alike on the flock and on the pastor, has noticed his misery. A warning severely given by means of a secret punishment, calling the delinquent to order, will prevent him from pursuing with impunity his reckless life. Would you have a public scandal, or would you leave unpunished either the faults that prove the unworthiness of him who commits them, or his want of the spirit of faith and his unwillingness to serve the faithful?" [40]

[39] *Praxis Fori Ecclesiastici,* p. 235.

[40] Peries, "Suspension ex Informata Conscientia"—*ER,* XV (1896), 9.

CHAPTER III

CONTROVERSIES IN THE DEVELOPMENT OF THE SUSPENSION *EX INFORMATA CONSCIENTIA*

THE more important data in the general historical outlook in the development of this power of proceeding *ex informata conscientia* have already been pointed out. It remains to be seen how the particular extent and limitations of this suspension have developed since the Council of Trent, which, as has been said, instituted this power in rather vague phraseology, until the present time, when the Code gives it in very precise wording. It is not the purpose here to follow up all the decisions of the Sacred Congregation, because they have been many and diverse, but only to examine those which have an influence on the development of this law, and which help in some way more fully to understand present legislation.

Perhaps the most bitterly contested phase of this question is grouped around the words of the Council *etiam ob occultum crimen.* In principle canonists have been almost unanimous in stating that the suspension *ex informata conscientia* could be applied only for occult crimes, and not for public crimes; however, a close study of these authors reveals that *de facto* they will admit a suspension *ex informata conscientia* for public crimes, in view of their rather flexible definition of occult. Bouix however insists on the principle that a suspension *ex informata conscientia* can be pronounced also for certain public crimes. A thorough study of his opinion on this question, together with a minute comparison of it with the view of the other canonists shows that practically Bouix agrees with the other canonists, although theoretically he takes just the contrary stand; his position has often been condemned, and he has been accused of being an extremist; however fundamentally Bouix had the correct principle and developed it logically, although he may have been guilty of rather exaggerated terminology at times.[1]

[1] Bouix is not however an extremist; the extreme view that all crimes, even notorious, are included in this suspension *ex informata conscientia* is advanced unblushingly by R. de M., *Institutiones Juris Canonici,* p. 506: his attempts to refute the saner view of other canonists are puerile.

Bouix maintains that in principle the suspension *ex informata conscientia* can be imposed also for public crimes. He admits that his position is unique. *"Fateor tamen, praeter laudatum Praesulem*[2] *nullum mihi occurrisse canonistam, qui praepositam difficultatem ex professo expenderit, et dictam facultatem Episcopis expresse, in casu publici delicti adscriptserit."*[3]

No one denies that the Council of Trent could have given the Bishops the power to proceed *ex informata conscientia* also in the case of public crimes, were that its intention. In examining the intention of the Council it will be well to keep uppermost in mind that the Council wishes this extrajudicial procedure to be an exceptional measure, and to touch only those cases that could not be reached by the ordinary procedure. Public crimes could ordinarily be satisfactorily handled by the judicial procedure, then existing: consequently the Council of Trent intended only to include the exceptional cases under this extrajudicial procedure.[4] The Council of Trent has clearly pointed out that it did not wish to abrogate existing legislation for the procedure in punishing crime,[5] but only to give an additional remedy for those things which were beyond the scope of the existing procedure. If this fundamental idea of the nature of this extrajudicial procedure as an EXTRAORDINARY measure is kept constantly in mind, it will be possible to discern the cases to which this procedure is to be applied.

Canonists on both sides of the question used the wording of the Council of Trent as the basis of their argumentation. In view of

[2] He refers to Monseigneur L'Evêque de Lucon, who writes: *"Ce mot (etiam) implique donc dans le premier cas 'même pour un crime occulte' toutes les espèces de crimes occultes, de quelque nature qu'ils soient; mais il implique à plus forte raison les crimes, qui sont notoires de quelque notorieté, que se soit, les crimes publics, ceux qui sont de nature à devenir notoire ou publics; même les le droit ou de fait: en un mot, toutes espèce de crime imaginable."—Des Sentences épiscopales dites de conscience informée*, Pars II, § 32. That this view is exaggerated is evident. Cf. Kober, Die Suspension, p. 70.

[3] Bouix, *De Judiciis*, II, 326.

[4] Cf. Kober, *Die Suspension*, p. 71.

[5] The famous Canon *"Qualiter et Quando"* of the Fourth Lateran Council was to remain in force for the ordinary procedure in criminal disciplinary matters.—Council of Trent, Sess. XXIV, de reform, cap. 5. Cf. also Kober, *Die Suspension*, p. 71.

the very involved wording of this law, an answer to this question should not be sought from the wording, but from the authentic interpretation which the Holy See has given to the law. However, it is necessary for completeness briefly to outline the arguments on each side.

Bouix argues from the formula *etiam ob occultum crimen:* "From this formula it seems conclusively to follow that the Bishop can do the same for an occult crime, as for a public crime. For where something is affirmed concerning some species with the particle *etiam,* the affirmation applies, even more strongly, to all other species in as far as the grammatical construction indicates. . . Thus, for example, if a person received the faculty of absolving from cases, *etiam episcopo reservatis, a fortiori,* he has the faculty of absolving from cases not reserved. Therefore from the fact that the extrajudicial faculty of suspension was conceded *ETIAM ob occultum crimen,* it follows that it was conceded *ob crimen non occultum,* or for the public crimes." [6]

De Angelis in refuting this opinion of Bouix, begins by stating that Bouix finds an argument where all former canonists have found only difficulty.[7] He continues with an argument *ad hominem* against Bouix, stating that the particle *etiam* is repeated in the Tridentine law, *etiam ob occultum crimen . . . etiam extrajudicialiter.* He says Bouix will certainly want to consider the second *etiam* redundant, otherwise the whole sense of the law would be subverted; but if he wishes to consider the second *etiam* redundant, he must likewise consider the first *etiam* redundant; now if this is conceded, then it follows that the law refers only to occult crimes. Droste-Messmer agrees with De Angelis in giving the meaning *id est* to *etiam:* "The Particle *etiam* in the Tridentine decree has not an extensive, but a restrictive meaning like the word *scilicet,* namely." [8]

Palmieri has perhaps offered the best explanation of the text of the Council of Trent in regard to this question. He explains that the decree after speaking of a cleric being prohibited to advance to orders for any cause whatever, e. g., lack of knowledge, adds that

[6] *De Judiciis,* II, 330.

[7] *Praelectiones Juris Canonici,* IV, I, 1.

[8] *Canonical Procedure,* 158.

he may also be prohibited on account of an occult crime. The *etiam* therefore in this case means something more than the usual causes for prohibiting the person to advance to orders, and this added reason is an occult crime. In the second part of the phrase another *etiam* appears, and this too has its proper meaning, and is seen to be parallel with the first *etiam.* In this case, after stating that the Bishop could proceed in this prohibition in any manner whatever, namely by the existing methods, he adds that he can do this also extrajudicially. In the latter case, therefore, as in the former, the *etiam* is used to denote something added to the existing legislation, and the meaning is clearly brought out by this parallelism, namely, that the *etiam ob occultum crimen* is parallel with the *etiam extrajudicialiter.* Therefore he concludes that in this decree a new power is given to the Bishops to proceed against occult crimes extrajudicially.[9]

After having analyzed the wording of the text of the law itself, it will be well to point out its interpretation through the centuries. In the seventeenth century there is the testimony of Fagnanus applying this law only to occult crimes.[10] In the following century Benedict XIV does not explicitly say that public crimes are not within the scope of the Tridentine measure, but from various passages in his writings it seems that he held that the suspension *ex informata conscientia* could be inflicted only for occult crimes. In his

[9] *Concilium Tridentinum . . . statuit ut clericus ab ascensu interdictus vel suspensus quacumque ex causa, puta ob defectum scientiae, aetatis, . . . vel propter aliquod delictum sive grave sive leve, addit (atque id novum est) etiam ob occultum crimen, interdictus vero aut suspensus quomodolibet, puta instituto judicio . . . addit: etiam extrajudicialiter . . . Heic porro adverte, illa vero duo incisa (etiam ob occultum crimen—etiam extrajudicialiter) sibi mutuo respondere alterumque ab altero exigi; cum autem dictum est, posse clericum interdici vel suspendi etiam ob occultum crimen, oportuit profecto addere, etiam extrajudicialiter; hoc alterum ex priori necessario consequitur . . . Ergo illud etiam quod auxesim notat, novam nempe supraaddictam potestatem, non est otiosum nec redundat. Ergo . . . illud etiam non infert alias species criminum circa quas versari valeat memorata potestas; sed infert, praeter alias causas interdicendi aut suspendendi jam ex jure notas aliosque modos pariterque cognitos, hanc quoque praesto esse, nempe crimen occultum, quod idcirco extrajudicialiter plectatur.* Vis Particulae Etiam in c. 1, Sess. XIV Conc. Trid. de Reform.—*Analecta Ecclesiastica,* II (1894), 497.

[10] *Commentarium in V Libros Decretalium,* in cap. *Ex Tenore.*

commentary on the text of this decree of the Council of Trent, he begins as follows: "*Ex quibus verbis colligitur, posse episcopun ob occultum crimen, etiam extrajudicialiter, etc.*"[11] It will be noted that in paraphrasing the text of Trent, Benedict XIV avoids the difficulty of explaining *etiam* and simply drops that word from his explanation; later, when referring to the impossibility of appeal from a suspension *ex informata conscientia,* he speaks only of *ob occultum delictum;* from these and similar passages it seems that it was the opinion of Benedict XIV that this suspension applied to occult crimes only. This conclusion is emphasized by the juxtaposition of the words *ob occultum crimen* and *sive ex informata conscientia* in the Constitution *Ad Militantes* of Benedict XIV issued on April 1, 1742.[12]

The Sacred Congregation of the Council has given several replies in which this question has been at least implicitly treated. All authors refer to the case of St. Agatha of the Goths of Feb. 26, 1853. The case is as follows: Oct. 13, 1851, Peter D'Ambrose, for reasons known to the Bishop, was suspended *ex informata conscientia* from the dignity of archpriest and likewise from the care of souls. The suspension was indefinite, not specifying any limitation of time. On recourse to the Holy See, the action of Bishop of St. Agatha was attacked, (1) because the suspension was inflicted for an indefinite period of time, and (2) because the Bishop did not have the faculty to suspend *ex informata conscientia* since the crime was public. The question was proposed, *an constet de validitate suspensionis in casu?* The Sacred Congregation replied, *nagative, salvo jure episcopo procedendi prout de jure.*[13] From this reply authors have concluded that the Bishop cannot suspend *ex informata conscientia* for public crimes. Bouix controverts this conclusion of authors:

> *Sacra Congregatio id unum pronuntiavit non constare de validitate dictae suspensionis; sed nullatcnus declaravit qua de causa ita judicaverit. Unde gratis assereretur causam hujus decisionis fuisse, quod delictum non fuerit occultum.*[14]

[11] *De Synodo Dioecesana,* Lib. 12, c. 1, n. 3.

[12] *Fontes,* n. 326.

[13] *Thesaurus Resolutionum,* CXII, 46; *ASS,* VII, 574; Pallottini, *Collectio Resolutionum S. C. C.,* sub verbo *Suspensio,* XVI, n. 161.

[14] *De Judiciis,* II, 331.

In view of the history of this question up to the time of Bouix, it seems that Bouix cannot be condemned for the attitude he took.

The authors, favoring the opinion that this suspension could be used only for occult crimes, drew an argument from a decision of the Sacred Congregation of the Council in 1873. A certain priest, whose name was not given was tried and convicted of a crime of immorality by the Bishop's consistory in the absence of the Bishop. After the priest had appealed from this sentence, the Bishop on Sept. 11, 1872, suspended him *ex informata conscientia,* in order to prevent further legal delays and to prevent possible scandal from the litigation. The case was taken to the Sacred Congregation and the suspension *ex informata conscientia* was overruled. *"Sacra Congregatio concilii causa cognita die 20 Dec. 1873, rescribere censuit: Decretum ex informata conscientia in casu non obstare quominus procedatur in causa appellationis prout, et quatenus et coram quo de jure."* [15] To this the editor of the *Acta* added: *"Ex quibus colliges: . . . 4. Decretum Suspensionis ex informata conscientia ob crimina publica editum non sustineri."* [16] It will be seen at once that the conclusion which has been drawn from this decision is not a necessary conclusion, and not warranted from the wording of the decision. Since the action of the Bishop attempting to suspend a priest *ex informata conscientia,* pending an appeal, was beyond the limits of his jurisdiction, and his action was an *attentatum,* the Holy See naturally annulled this suspension *ex informata conscientia.* Whether the publicity of the crime was a basis for its decision is not explicitly mentioned. The importance of this case becomes evident when it is remembered that it is explicitly referred to in the Instruction of the Sacred Congregation of Bishops and Regulars in 1880 as a precedent for future legislation.

In this Instruction the Sacred Congregation says: *"Plenam quoque vim servat suam extrajudiciale remedium ex informata conscientia pro criminibus occultis, quod decrevit S. Trident. Syn-*

[15] S. C. C., *Bosnien et Sirmien,* 20 dec. 1873—*ASS,* VII, 575; cf. also *AKKR,* XLVII (1895), 155-160.

[16] *ASS,* VII, 575.

odus."[17] The same is maintained in the Instruction of the Sacred Congregation of the Propagation of the Faith: *"Suspensioni ex informata conscientia justam ac legitimam causam praebet crimen, seu culpa a suspenso commissa. Haec autem debet occulta, et ita gravis, ut talem promereatur punitionem.*"[18]

In spite of this consistent insistence of the Sacred Congregation that the suspension *ex informata conscientia* can be inflicted only for occult crimes, the Sacred Congregation in several instances has sustained decisions in which the suspension was inflicted for public crimes. Cavagnis cites the case of Charles Passaglia, an ex-Jesuit.[19] In 1863 many rebellious priests in Italy, headed by Passaglia, started a movement antagonistic to the temporal sovereignty of the Holy See. They wanted Pius IX to renounce all claims to his possessions in Italy and to acknowledge Victor Emmanuel as the lawful head of the Italian peninsula. By their action these priests thus incurred the censures decreed by Pius V in his Instruction *Admonet Nos.*[20] Here was a case of open conflict between the Church and the State, and the Bishops fearing the intervention or prevention of the civil power, dared not prosecute these priests according to the ordinary canonical procedure. Seeing no other way of handling the situation, the Bishops made use of the power granted them by the Council of Trent, and suspended these priests *ex informata conscientia.* On recourse to the Holy See, the Sacred Congregation of the Council sustained the suspension. Here evidently there is not a case of an occult crime, but of a national uprising in which many priests committed a very grave public offense: yet in spite of all this the suspension was upheld. The importance and historical significance of this and similar cases will be summarized after a few similar cases have been mentioned.

The Bishop of Lucon received very discouraging reports about the conditions of a certain Peveteau, an irremovable pastor in his diocese. At first the Bishop warned and admonished him, but to no

[17] Instr. S. C. EE et RR, 11 iun. 1880, art. 9,—*Fontes,* n. 2005; cf. also S. C. C., *Patavina,* 11 sept. 1880, *ASS,* XIV, 292; *Thesaurus Resolutionum,* CXXXIX, 587.

[18] 20 oct. 1884—*Collectanea,* n. 1628.

[19] *Institutiones Juris Publici,* II, 43.

[20] 29 mart. 1567—*Fontes,* n. 119.

avail. More than ten witnesses were called to testify concerning the character of the priest; these witnesses refused to testify in court, fearing the vengeance of Peveteau; on May 25, 1846 the Bishop suspended Peveteau *ex informata conscientia.* Peveteau disregarded the suspension and continued to exercise his sacred functions. Whereupon on June 24 the Ordinary publicly declared Peveteau suspended and irregular. The priest appealed to the Metropolitan who refused to give a definite answer. The case was then taken to the Holy See. To the question, *an suspensio lata ex informata conscientia sustineatur in casu,* the Sacred Congregation replied, *affirmative ad formam cap. 1 Sess. XIV, de ref.*[21]

A similar case was upheld by the same Congregation in 1795. Bernard Palanghius had been suspended *ex informata conscientia* by the Bishop of Perugia, for several crimes. More than twenty witnesses had testified in the case, and to all appearances it was a public crime. Nevertheless the Sacred Congregation sustained the suspension *ex informata conscientia* which the Bishop imposed upon Palanghius.[22]

A confirmatory argument for the possibility of the use of the suspension *ex informata conscientia* in certain public cases can be drawn from a decision of the Sacred Congregation of Bishops and Regulars in 1894. In 1892 Olympius Zill de Silles, a French priest, was given a position on the Seminary faculty in the diocese of St. Joseph in Costa Rica. He was likewise made chaplain of a sisters' convent. In view of internal discord, the Bishop deemed it necessary to relieve Father De Silles of his position on the faculty. Later the Sisters requested his removal from his chaplaincy; the petition was forwarded both to the Bishop and to the French Consul. After the Bishop had removed him, De Silles threatened retaliation in the public press. Disregarding the threat of suspension, the priest published several articles of a scandalous nature. Thereupon the Bishop suspended him *ex informata conscientia.* Recourse was had to the Holy See; the Bishop offered as the reason for the suspension

[21] S. C. C., *Lucionen.*, 8 apr. 1848—*ASS,* XIV, 299; *Thesaurus Resolutionum,* CVIII, 135-165; Pallottini, *Collectio Resolutionum S. C. C.*, sub verbo *Suspensio,* XVI, n. 138.

[22] S. C. C., *Perusina,* 26 sept. 1795—*Thesaurus Resolutionum,* LXIV, 196; Pallottini, *Collectio Resolutionum S. C. C.*, sub verbo *Suspensio,* XVI, n. 167.

ex informata conscientia, the damage done to the sisters, and the public scandal; the priest protested the suspension on the basis that his crime was public and that a trial was possible. After carefully considering the case, the Sacred Congregation replied to the proposed question, *an et quomodo sustineatur suspensio inflicta in casu,* by sustaining the suspension, *attentis omnibus in casu concurrentibus, affirmative in omnibus.*[23] Here again there is a case of the suspension *ex informata conscientia* being sustained even though the crime was public.

Viewing on the one hand the constant position of the Sacred Congregations on the theory that the Tridentine suspension *ex informata conscientia* may be imposed only for occult crimes, and on the other hand the decisions of the same Congregations sustaining suspensions *ex informata conscientia* which have been inflicted for public crimes, the first thought that would suggest itself is the seeming contradiction between the theory and the practice on this question. To explain this seeming contradiction satisfactorily has been one of the stumbling blocks of canonists who wrote before the promulgation of the Code. All canonists have recognized the fact that the contradiction is only seeming, and that *de facto,* the Sacred Congregation would not maintain one thing in theory and something quite different in practice. The method which practically all canonists have taken to explain this difficulty away centers about their definition of the term OCCULT. It is unnecessary to quote the various definitions which canonists have offered to cover this case; in general it can be said that before the Code they defined occult as something which could not be proved in a judicial trial, either due to physical or moral impossibility.[24]

Contrary to this rather common method of defining the word "occult," Bouix gave the definition which was later to be embodied into Code legislation. He admits that the suspension *ex informata conscientia,* decreed by the Council of Trent, is ordinarily designed to cover occult crimes which could not be reached by an ordinary judicial procedure. But he states further that in a few rare exceptional cases the suspension *ex informata conscientia* may be inflicted

[23] S. C. EE et RR, 24 aug. 1894—*ASS,* XXVII, 430.

[24] Cf. Hinschius, *System des Kathol. Kirchenrechts,* V, 610.

for a public crime. He emphasizes however the fact that this suspension *ex informata conscientia* is an extraordinary remedy, and is to be used only in those cases, "*qui ex speciali causa tale remedium requirunt, et in quibus non posset, absque notabili boni publici damno, via ordinaria procedi.*" [25] Here then Bouix arrives at the same conclusion which the other canonists had reached, namely that the suspension *ex informata conscientia* can be imposed only when a judicial process is physically or morally impossible. In spite of all the adverse criticism he has received on account of the position he maintained on this question, Bouix' opinion has been adopted by the Code in canon 2191, which admits the possibility of the application of the suspension *ex informata conscientia* in a few public cases. Thus this question, which has agitated canonists for many years, has been definitely settled by the Code.

The difficulty of properly understanding the *etiam ob occultum crimen* has been one of the greatest worries of canonists treating of the suspension *ex informata conscientia.* It was necessary to give considerable space to this question in view of its historical importance, in determining the causes for which a suspension *ex informata conscientia* could be imposed. It will be sufficient if the other points of interest in the particular development of this legislation are but cursorily mentioned.

The Council of Trent does not mention whether the suspension *ex informata conscientia* can be perpetual or only temporary. One of the earliest decisions of the Sacred Congregation of the Council interpreted the Tridentine suspension as applying to both temporal and perpetual suspensions: "*Congregatio Concilii censuit c. 1, Sess. XIV, de ref., habere locum in suspensionibus et prohibitionibus tam temporalibus, quam perpetuis, et temporalem prohibitionem et suspensionem dici eam, ubi ex delicto occulto extrajudicialiter procedit episcopus, ad suum beneplacitum prohibendo vel suspendendo.*" [26] Later decisions of the Sacred Congregation reversed the decision on this point and allowed the suspension only for a time, and not *in perpetuum.*[27] In the Instruction of the Sacred Congregation

[25] *De Judiciis,* II, 344.

[26] S. C. C., *Nullius,* 3 feb. 1593—*Fontes,* n. 2254.

[27] S. C. C., *S. Severini,* 17 sept. 1778—*Thesaurus Resolutionum,* XLVII, 47; *ASS,* XIV, 412; Pierantonelli, *Praxis Fori Ecclesiastici,* n. 21; S. C. C.,

of the Propagation of the Faith of Oct. 20, 1884, the Bishop is forbidden to impose this suspension *in perpetuum*. The Code preserves this regulation in c. 2188, without determining whether this regulation is for validity or only for liceity.

That there can be no appeal from the suspension *ex informata conscientia* is evident from the wording of the Tridentine decree, "*nulla contra ipsius praelati voluntatem concessa licentia de se promoveri faciendo aut ad priores ordines, gradus dignitates sive honores restitutio suffragetur.*" [28] The Sacred Congregation has insisted upon this in many decisions. A Bishop suspended a pastor *ex causis sibi notis*, and this pastor appealed to the Metropolitan; the case was referred to the Holy See and the Sacred Congregation replied: *Ab hujusmodi suspensione non dari appelationem et parochum, qui sacramenta ut supra ministravit, irregularitatem contraxisse.*[29] Similarly in 1654 the Sacred Congregation replied to the question, *An ordinariis locorum vigore facultatis sibi concessae a S. Concilio Tridentino, Sess. XIV, c. 1, de ref., liceat ob legitimas causas suspendere etiam extrajudicialiter clericos et presbyteros saeculares, etiam parochos sibi subditos, sublata eis facultate appellandi,* that the Bishops did have the power.[30] It has been, therefore, the unanimous teaching of canonists that there is no appeal from an extrajudicial suspension, which the Bishop inflicts in virtue of the power given him by the first chapter of the fourteenth session of the Council of Trent. That recourse may be had to the Holy See is evident.

Concerning the manner of giving this extrajudicial suspension nothing was decided by the Council itself. The present definite manner as outlined in the Code is based very largely on the Instruction of the Sacred Congregation of the Propagation of the Faith, given Oct. 20, 1884, to which reference has been made several times

Placentina, 26 feb. 1848—*Thesaurus Resolutionum*, CVIII, 49; S. C. C., *S. Agathae Gothorum*, 26 feb. 1853—*Thesaurus Resolutionum*, CVIII, 49; CXII, 46; S. C. C., *Galtellin.*, 20 mart. 1880—*Thesaurus Resolutionum*, CXXXIX, 166.

[28] Conc. Trid., Sess. XIV, cap. 1, de reform.

[29] S. C. C., *Sagonen.*, 21 iun. 1623—*Fontes*, n. 2442.

[30] S. C. C., *Bononien.*, 14 nov. 1654—*Fontes*, n. 2741.

above. This instruction for the first time gives a complete and succinct summary of all the legislation on the extrajudicial suspension of the Council of Trent. It is based upon previous decisions, which are scattered here and there in the history of this legislation. As early as 1643 the Sacred Congregation decided that the Bishop did not have to manifest the cause of the suspension to the person upon whom it was inflicted.[31] However it has been the constant teaching of doctors that in giving this suspension, the Bishop must express the fact that he is acting in virtue of the power given him by the Council of Trent, Sess. XIV, cap. 1, de reform., or that it is a suspension *ex informata conscientia,* or that it is given for causes known to himself. The expression of this is necessary so that the suspended person may know that he cannot appeal to the Metropolitan from this suspension, but that the only defense left to him is to have recourse to the Holy See. Formerly it was held that this extrajudicial suspension was not valid if it was not in writing.[32] This is likewise the purport of the Instruction of 1884: *"Hujusmodi praeceptum semper in scriptis intimandum est, die ac mense designato; ideoque autem fieri debet vel ab ipso ordinario, vel ab alia pèrsona de expresso ipsius mandato."* [33] The present legislation likewise favors writing, but does not demand it for the validity of the suspension.

HISTORICAL SUMMARY

A BRIEF history of the extrajudicial suspension has been attempted. It has been the purpose of these chapters to point out the salient features in that history, not in order to give a complete historical narrative of this extrajudicial procedure, but simply to give the facts which will render a study of the present legislation more complete and more intelligible. At different periods in the Church's history different modes of procedure have been in vogue.

[31] *"Ordinarium si suspendat aliquem vigore c. 1, Sess. XIV, de reform., non teneri exprimere delictum, seu causam suspensionis ipsi reo, sed tantum Sedi Apostolicae, ad quam reus recursum habuerit."* S. C. C., *Vercellen.,* 21 mart. 1643—*Fontes,* n. 2642.

[32] S. C. C., 11 aug. 1883—*Analecta Juris Pontificii,* XX, 84.

[33] *Collectanea,* N. 1628.

The Church, the divine custodian of faith and morals, has ever been alert to the changing needs of her children. She has realized that the primary requisite in carrying out her divine ministry of sanctifying all men is to have her priests spotless and without offense. Like a kind mother, she has looked with special solicitude to those of her children who are called to a more eminent position. She has left nothing undone to make her chosen ministers the light of the world.

After centuries of gradual perfection, she gave the world the marvelous procedure which is found in the Decretals. Before any crime could be punished, a canonical trial to prove the guilt of the accused party was necessary and at this trial the accused was given every weapon to prove his innocence, if innocent he was. In the sixteenth century the pristine spirit of faith and fervor had yielded in many things to a spirit of worldliness, pride and ambition. Unworthy candidates sought admission to the sanctuary and unworthy priests at times defiled their sacred trust. By means of various legal technicalities, some of these unworthy men were able to elude with impunity the judicial processes which were necessary. The Bishops often found themselves helpless to remedy such evils. With alarm the Holy Fathers of Trent beheld in the midst of the clergy evils, the removal of which was essential to the fulfillment of the divine command to sanctify all men. Consequently they decreed that the Bishops must rid the sanctuary of such men and, if this was impossible according to the existing juridical procedure, then the Bishops should proceed extrajudicially and even for occult crimes. Such a tremendous and seemingly tyrannical power caused a consternation in the Church. The conservatism of the Church seemed to be a thing of the past and men stood in awe at the almost arbitrary power of the Bishop. Opposition developed. Slowly the Sacred Congregation interpreted this decree of the Council of Trent, and gradually men began to realize the utility, the necessity, of this extrajudicial means of procedure. However, it was only after an express declaration of Pius VI that to deny this power of the Bishops was to go counter to the ecclesiastical authority, that peace was established. But even this did not make the law popular. Its continued unpopularity may to some extent be attributed to the abuse, by which some Bishops certainly violated justice in applying this extraordinary remedy; but to a large extent its unpopularity was due to a lack of a comprehensive understanding of the measure, to a fear of an unknown evil. The words of the Council of Trent were vague and, although the Sacred Congregation had on numerous occasions given very definite decisions, the need for a complete statement of the law was felt. To answer this need the Sacred Congregation of the Propagation of the Faith on Oct. 20, 1884, issued the Instruction to which reference has been made. In this Instruction the Sacred Congregation in a very clear and concise manner gives the complete legislation on the extrajudicial procedure, commonly called the suspension *ex informata conscientia.* The Code, with but slight modifications, has taken over this legislation of the Instruction. A full interpretation of the present legislation will be offered in the second part of this work.

PART II

PRESENT LEGISLATION

CHAPTER IV

THE POWER TO SUSPEND *EX INFORMATA CONSCIENTIA*

Canon 2186. § 1. Ordinariis licet ex informata conscientia clericos suos suspendere ab officio sive ex parte sive etiam in totum.

§ 2. Extraordinarium hoc remedium adhibere non licet, si Ordinarius potest sine gravi incommodo ad juris normam in subditum procedere.

In this first canon of the title dealing with the subject under consideration, is laid down the general power which the Ordinary has to suspend his clerical subjects *ex informata conscientia*. In the first part of this work it has been shown that this power was given to Bishops for the first time by the Council of Trent.[1] Before the Council of Trent, in order to punish a cleric, a Bishop was obliged to follow the regular judicial procedure established for criminal matters.[2] The power was not clearly defined in its Tridentine expression; hence successive declarations and decisions of the Holy See were necessary to clarify its extension and interpretation. The first complete codification of the existing legislation on this subject was given by the Sacred Congregation of the Propagation in 1884; in this instruction the Sacred Congregation outlined in detail this extrajudicial procedure, as it was to be followed in missionary countries.[3] The norms, set down in this Instruction, were accepted as interpretative guides in countries not subject to the Congregation of the Propagation of the Faith. With some modifications, these norms are accepted by the Code, and thus receive the sanction of universal legislation.

The first paragraph of canon 2186 states that Ordinaries are allowed to suspend *ex informata conscientia* clerics, who are subject to them. For a full interpretation of this canon it is necessary to determine the scope or object of this suspension; those vested with

[1] Conc. Trid. Sess. XIV, cap. 1 de reform.

[2] C. 1, C. II, q. 1; c. 4, X, *De Temporibus Ordinationum,* I, 11.

[3] *Collectanea,* n. 1628.

authority to use it; and those upon whom this authority may be exercised.

The second paragraph of this canon explicitly declares that this suspension is an extraordinary remedy, which can be used only when it is impossible without a grave inconvenience to proceed according to the norm of law.

Article I—The Object

It has been pointed out that a twofold power was given to Bishops by the Council of Trent: first, to forbid a person to ascend to higher orders; and secondly, to suspend a cleric from orders already received.[4] In spite of the fact that this twofold power to proceed extrajudicially was granted by this decree, from a very early time both powers have been understood under the expression 'suspension *ex informata conscientia*'. The power to interdict or forbid a person to receive orders is no longer comprehended under the term 'suspension *ex informata conscientia*'. Code legislation has separated these powers, and treats them separately.

In canon 970 the power of the Ordinary to prohibit the advance to orders is mentioned. The Bishop or religious superior is given the power to prohibit, even extrajudicially, the advance of any candidate to orders for any canonical cause whatever, even for an occult crime. From such a decree of the Bishop or religious superior the candidate can, of course, have recourse to the Holy See. Canon 2222, § 2 likewise refers to this power of the Ordinary.[5] Canon 970 evidently reiterates the Tridentine decree by which Bishops are allowed to preceed *ex informata conscientia*, or extrajudicially, in forbidding their subjects to ascend to higher orders, even though the cause be occult.[6] It will not be useless to remark that the canon says *clericis suis;* there is no reason to include lay people as the passive subject

[4] Sess. XIV, cap. 1 de reform.; cf. also Hinschius, *Kathol. Kirchenrechts*, V, 609; Molitor, *Kanonisches Gerichtsverfahren*, p. 221; Kober, *Die Suspension*, p. 65; Peries, *La Procédure Canonique*, p. 174.

[5] Canon 970 grants this power for any canonical cause while canon 2191 grants it only for a crime. Cf. Wernz-Vidal, *Jus Canonicum*, VI, n. 794.

[6] Cf. Benedict XIV, Const. *Ad Militantes*, 1 apr. 1742—*Fontes*, n. 326; S. C. C., *Vercellen.*, 21 mart. 1643—*Fontes*, n. 2642; S. C. C., *Alerien.*, 24 nov. 1657—*Fontes*, n. 2752.

of this prohibition, since the Bishop's power over them is sufficiently stressed in the previous canons, where the necessity of the call of the Bishop is intimated.[7]

In canon 2186 the power of the Ordinary to proceed *ex informata conscientia* is therefore limited to the case of suspension, and a particular suspension, namely, the suspension from office. The word 'suspension' in canonical phraseology means the prohibition to use some power, or to exercise a right, or to receive the fruits of a benefice. A suspension has a twofold use, and may be either a censure [8] or a vindictive penalty.[9] A suspension does not mean the withdrawal or removal from an office or benefice. There are two general classes of suspensions, suspension *ab officio* and suspension *a beneficio*. The suspension *ex informata conscientia* is concerned only with the suspension *ab officio,* which is defined as a prohibition, forbidding every act both of the power of orders and jurisdiction and also of the administration of an office, with the exception of the administration of the goods of one's own benefice.[10] In order to understand the scope of the suspension *ex informata conscientia,* it is necessary to remember the exact meaning of the suspension *ab officio*.[11] The word *officium* [12] in this matter is to be taken in the meaning evidently intended by canons 2256, § 1 and 2279, § 1,[13] and not in the strict sense of an *officium* as defined elsewhere in the code.[14] A general

[7] Cf. C. 968, § 1; Suarez, *De Remotione Parochorum,* p. 217.

[8] CC. 2255, 2278.

[9] C. 2298, 2°.

[10] *"Suspensio ab officio simpliciter, nulla adiecta limitatione, vetat omnem actum tum potestatis ordinis et jurisdictionis, tum etiam merae administrationis ex officio competentis, excepta administratione bonorum proprii beneficii."*—C. 2279, § 1.

[11] Cf. Vermeersch-Creusen, *Epitome,* III, n. 482; Sole, *De Delictis et Poenis,* p. 143.

[12] "By the name of divine offices are understood functions of the power of orders, which by institution of Christ or the Church are ordinated to divine cult, and which can be performed only by clerics."—C. 2256, § 1.

[13] *"Officii appellatione omnis potestas spiritualis significatur; eaque duo continentur, ordo et jurisdictio; quo circa haec suspensio potest esse vel ab ordine solum, vel solum a jurisdictione, vel ab utroque."*—D'Annibale, *Summa Theologiae Moralis,* I, n. 381.

[14] C. 145; cf. also Wernz-Vidal, *Jus Canonicum,* II, n. 140; Chelodi, *Jus de Personis,* n. 131; Vermeersch-Creusen, *Epitome,* I, n. 227.

suspension *ab officio* prohibits every act of the power of orders and jurisdiction and likewise every act of administration of an office, except the administration of one's own benefice.

In inflicting this suspension *ex informata conscientia* the Ordinary may inflict it totally, and then the suspension is understood in the sense just explained, or he may inflict a partial suspension. However in the latter case he must specify the acts prohibited.[15] The code itself specifies the various partial suspensions *ab officio* and indicates what acts are forbidden by each:

C. 2279. § 2. *Suspensio*:

1°. *A Jurisdictione generatim, vetat omnem actum potestatis jurisdictionis pro utroque foro tam ordinariae quam delegatae;*

2°. *A divinis, omnem actum potestatis ordinis quam quis sive per sacram ordinationem sive per privilegium obtinet;*

3°. *Ab ordinibus, omnem actum potestatis ordinis receptae per ordinationem;*

4°. *A sacris ordinibus, omnem actum potestatis ordinis receptae per ordinationem in sacris;*

5°. *A certo et definito ordine exercendo, omnem actum ordinis designati; suspensus autem prohibetur insuper eundem ordinem conferre et superiorem recipere receptumque post suspensionem exercere;*

6°. *A certo et definito ordine conferendo ipsum ordinem conferre, non vero inferiorem nec superiorem;*

7°. *A certo et definito ministerio, ex. gr., audiendi confessiones, vel officio, ex. gr., cum cura animarum, omnem actum eiusdem ministerii vel officii.*[16]

8°. *Ab ordine pontificali, omnem actum potestatis ordinis episcopalis;*

9°. *A pontificalibus, exercitium actuum pontificalium, ad normam can 337,* § 2.

If the Ordinary suspends *ab officio* simply, the suspension is concerned with every act of the power of orders, jurisdiction, and

[15] C. 2188, 3°.

[16] Since c. 880, § 2 gives the Ordinary the power to revoke faculties for a grave reason, it has been held that the Ordinary could not suspend from hearing confessions *ex informata conscientia.* The Ordinary however certainly has this power. Cf. Suarez, *De Remotione Parochorum,* p. 218; Vermeersch-Creusen, *Epitome,* III, n. 373; Muniz, *Procedimientos Eclesiasticos,* I, 717; S. C. C., *Perusina,* 24 sept. 1795, *Thesaurus Resolutionum,* LXIV, 196.

administration; if he does not wish to suspend totally, then the particular suspension is to be clearly indicated.

The Code therefore limits the Ordinary's power in proceeding *ex informata conscientia* to the suspension *ab officio.* Here there is question of a law dealing with the infliction of penalties, and consequently one which must be strictly interpreted, and not extended beyond the evident meaning of the text in the context.[17] The arguments advanced by some older canonists purporting to give this law a wider interpretation are not sufficient to carry conviction, or even to make the question doubtful.[18] The Ordinary would be acting wholly beyond his jurisdiction, and consequently invalidly, in attempting to impose excommunication, interdict, or any of the penal remedies by a decree *ex informata conscientia.*[19] The nullity of an act follows from the defect of anything which is essential to the act itself,[20] and certainly the power to inflict a suspension *ex informata conscientia* is essential to the validity of the suspension; consequently if that power is exceeded, and an attempt is made to extend it without jurisdiction, the resultant act of suspension is certainly invalid.[21]

The power to proceed *ex informata conscientia* likewise does not apply to suspension *a beneficio.*[22] This power was not given to Bishops by the decree of the Council of Trent, and has not since been given. The words of the Council of Trent are clear on this point, *ab ordinibus, seu gradibus vel dignitatibus;* obviously they do not include benefices. Further that an attempt to include the suspension from benefice under the suspension *ex informata conscientia* is foreign to the mind of the Council of Trent is evident from

[17] Cf. Wernz, *Jus Decretalium,* V, n. 895.

[18] Cf. Santi-Leitner, *Praelectiones Juris Canonici,* V, n. 21; Bourret, *Des Sentences Ecclésiastiques,* p. 63.

[19] Cf. Kober, *Die Suspension,* p. 69; Bouix, *De Judiciis,* II, 341; Wernz-Vidal, *Jus Canonicum,* VI, n. 800.

[20] C. 1680, § 1.

[21] Cf. Suarez, *De Remotione Parochorum,* p. 220; Noval, *De Processibus,* n. 895.

[22] Cf. Kober, *Die Suspension,* p. 69; Molitor, *Kanonisches Gerichtsverfahren,* p. 610; Richter, *Kirchenrecht,* II, 787; Droste-Messmer, *Canonical Procedure,* n. 96; Smith, *Elements of Ecclesiastical Law,* II, n. 1287; Wernz-Vidal, *Jus Canonicum,* VI, n. 800.

the clear distinction which is made between the suspension from office and the suspension from benefice in other decrees of the Council of Trent.[23] Due probably either to the lack of a clear understanding of the distinction between the suspension from office and the suspension from benefice, or else to a tendency to give the law of the Council of Trent an unduly wide interpretation, some authors held that the Ordinary could also inflict a suspension from benefice *ex informata conscientia*.[24] In view of the definition of these two modes of suspension by the Code [25] there can no longer be any doubt in the question.[26] Should an Ordinary so suspend one of his clerics, it is evident that the suspension would be invalid, and could be completely disregarded by the cleric even in the external forum.[27]

Article II—Active Subject

In instituting the suspension *ex informata conscientia* the Council of Trent uses the term *Praelatus*. This term was not clearly defined in pre-Code legislation. The decree of the Council of Trent evidently wished to impart this power to those who are to govern the Church, those who are responsible for the welfare both of the clergy and the laity.[28] Under this term the Bishops were primarily understood; likewise those who are in a similar position to Bishops, namely Vicars and Prefects Apostolic for mission countries, and Major

[23] Cf. Conc. Trid., Sess. XIV, de reform., cap. 6; Wernz-Vidal, *Jus Canonicum*, VI, n. 800.

[24] Two arguments are offered in particular for this view: since *beneficium est propter officium*, if the Ordinary can suspend from office, *a fortiori* he can suspend from benefice; secondly, *facultas concessa ad puniendum est res favorabilis*, and consequently is to be interpreted widely.—Santi, *Praelectiones Juris Canonici*. V, n. 21. These arguments are ably refuted by Bassibey, "Des Sentences ex Informata Conscientia,"—*JJC*, II (1893), 280; Bouix, *De Judiciis*, II, 355; Droste-Messmer, *Canonical Procedure*, n. 96.

[25] CC. 2279, 2280.

[26] Since the Code, no canonist supports the other opinion.

[27] Irregularity is not incurred by the exercise of powers, from which one has been suspended by an invalid suspension. Cf. Vering, *Droit Canon*, II, 450.

[28] The legislator had in mind analagous measures issued by Innocent III at the Fourth Lateran Council, 1215, when it imposed upon Prelates the obligation to repress the vices of their inferiors.—C. 13, X, *Irrefragabili*, I, 31.

Superiors of clerical exempt religious. Since the Vicar Capitular does not have all the rights of a Bishop, it was disputed whether this particular power could be exercised by him. Again there was considerable doubt, as to the extension of this power to Vicars General.

Benedict XIV already substituted the word *Episcopus* for Prelate.[29] In the Instruction of 1884, the Sacred Congregation generally uses the term *Praelati;* however in N. X it uses *Praesules,* and in N. XIII, quoting Benedict XIV, the term *Episcopus,* while in the Introduction it uses the term *Ordinarii.*[30]

Canon 2186 gives this power to Ordinaries, and the extension of the term no longer offers difficulty, because the term is defined by the Code.[31] This power belongs to the following:

1. Residential Bishops in their own territory. The Bishop is by divine right the guardian and shepherd of the flock entrusted to his care. His is the duty to correct the faults and defects of both the clergy and the laity; both the Law of the Decretals and the Council of Trent recognize in Bishops a very special duty to watch over the ecclesiastics who are subject to them.[32] He is to insure the good government of his diocese, by the cooperation of his clerics, and it is essential for him to correct his clerics and punish them if necessary. For this purpose he may find it not only useful but sometimes almost necessary to make use of his power to suspend *ex informata conscientia.*[33]

2. Abbots and Prefects Nullius. Although they do not necessarily have the episcopal character, their jurisdiction is very similar to that of residential Bishops.[34]

3. Vicars and Prefects Apostolic. For territories not erected into dioceses, the Vicars and Prefects Apostolic are appointed by the Holy See.[35] They have the same rights and faculties as residential Bishops,

[29] *De Synodo Dioecesana,* lib. XII, c. 8, n. 6.

[30] *Collectanea,* N. 1628.

[31] C. 198, § 1.

[32] C. 13, X, *Irrefragabili,* I, 31; Conc. Trid. Sess. VI, de reform., cap. 3; Sess. XIV, de reform., cap. 1; *Prooem.;* Sess. XXIV, de reform., cap. 3.

[33] Cavagnis, *Institutiones Juris Publici,* II, n. 63.

[34] CC. 319, § 1, 323, § 1.

[35] C. 293, § 1.

unless the Holy See restricts these rights;[36] often they have even more extensive delegated power than residential Bishops.[37] Among their rights and duties is that of correction and punishment.[38] Their right to proceed *ex informata conscientia* was recognized before the Code by the Instruction of 1884, "to the end that the Ordinaries of Catholic Missions proceed with precaution and safety in passing these sentences, the S. Congregation of the Propaganda has considered it useful to publish this present instruction, to which these same Ordinaries must conform in employing this extraordinary remedy." [39]

4. Apostolic Administrators. The government of a diocese is sometimes committed to Apostolic Administrators,[40] whose rights are coextensive either with the rights of a residential Bishop or with the rights of a Vicar Capitular,[41] according to the duration of the office.

5. Vicars Capitular, or as they are called in the United States, Administrators, appointed to govern the diocese in the event of the death, removal or transfer of a residential Bishop. The Vicar Capitular has the ordinary jurisdiction of a residential Bishop, both in spiritual and temporal affairs, in all things unless an exception is expressly made in law.[42] The law does not exempt the suspension *ex informata conscientia* from his powers; consequently there can be no doubt but that he has this power.[43]

6. Major Superiors of Clerical Exempt Religious. They are Ordinaries and exercise ordinary jurisdiction over their subjects also

[36] C. 294, § 1.

[37] Cf. Wernz, *Jus Decretalium,* II, n. 701.

[38] Cf. C. 296 and following canons.

[39] *Collectanea,* n. 1628.

[40] C. 312.

[41] C. 315, § 2, 1°.

[42] C. 435, § 1.

[43] Before the Code this question was disputed. Although this power was granted by most canonists, e.g., De Angelis, Lega, Heiner, Gasparri, etc.; still it was vigorously denied by Stremler and especially by Bassibey, "Des Sentences Ex Informata Conscientia"—*JJC,* II (1893), 343; other authors impressed by the strength of Bassibey's arguments advised the Vicar Capitular to refrain from the use of this power until the question be definitely settled. Cf. Wernz, *Jus Decretalium,* V, n. 892. Since the Code, this power cannot be denied.

in the external forum.[44] The following are Major Superiors: (a) Abbot Primate; (b) Abbot Superior of a Monastic Congregation. These two do not enjoy this power unless it is explicitly granted to them by the Constitutions or by a Decree of the Holy See.[45] (c) Abbot of an independent monastery; (d) Supreme Moderators; (e) Provincials; and (f) Vicars and others having the power *ad instar* of the Provincials.[46]

Since Major Superiors have ordinary jurisdiction over their subjects, and have the power to suspend them according to the norms of law, there is no reason to deny them the right to suspend their subjects likewise *ex informata conscientia.*[47]

7. Vicars General are likewise Ordinaries.[48] However, since they are forbidden to impose penalities without a special mandate,[49] it is evident that they do not have the power to suspend clerics *ex informata conscientia.*[50] A possible exception to this rule might arise if the Vicar General, while the Bishop is impeded in the government of the diocese, is appointed to govern the diocese.[51] In this case, he would enjoy this power, unless it were explicitly forbidden.[52] In any case however the Bishop can delegate this power to his Vicar General by special mandate; if then the Vicar General exercises this delegated power, in the decree of suspension itself, he must, for the validity of the decree, mention that he is acting in virtue of a special mandate.

[44] CC. 488, 2°, 4°, 501, § 1.

[45] C. 501, § 3.

[46] C. 488, 8°.

[47] Cf. De Angelis, *Praelectiones Juris Canonici,* V, 65; Giraldi, *Expositio Juris Pontificii,* Pars II, Sect. 43, n. 2; Arndt, "Die Suspension"—*AKKR,* 73 (1895), 143-144; Blat, *Commentarium,* IV, 704; Bizarri, *Collectanea,* p. 24.

[48] It was commonly admitted even before the Code that Vicars General did not have this power. Giraldi, *Expositio Juris Pontificii,* Pars II, Sect. 43, n. 2, thought the question was doubtful, while other canonists considered the matter settled. Cf. Bassibey, "Des Sentences Ex Informata Conscientia," *JJC,* II (1893), 355; Hinschius, *Kathol. Kirchenrechts,* II, 244 and V, 610.

[49] C. 2220, § 2.

[50] Cf. Vermeersch-Creusen, *Epitome,* III, n. 373; Bouuaert-Simenon, n. 1236, et omnes.

[51] C. 429, § 1.

[52] Cf. Wernz-Vidal, *Jus Canonicum,* VI, n. 797.

Article III—Passive Subject

The passive subjects of this suspension are clerics. In this matter, clerics must be understood as those who have received tonsure.[53] That clerics only can be the passive subjects of this suspension follows from the very nature of an ecclesiastical suspension.[54] A suspension *ex informata conscientia* can be inflicted only upon those clerics who are subject to the person inflicting it.[55] Consequently the Ordinary of the diocese can inflict it on the secular clergy who are subject to him, whether by incardination into his diocese,[56] or by reason of having domicile or quasidomicile in his diocese.[57] Non-exempt religious are likewise subject to the Local Ordinary, and may be proceeded against by a suspension *ex informata conscientia*. The power of the Local Ordinary concerning exempt religious is very limited; he can however suspend them *ex informata conscientia* from hearing confessions, in as far as they have received faculties from him.[58] It is well to remember also that the Bishops and Prefects Apostolic have the right to recall missionaries and regular pastors, either for unfitness or for delinquency in the administration of the sacraments, even without consulting the regular Superiors, and regular Superiors can recall their subjects without consulting the Bishop or Prefect Apostolic.[59] Such procedure is not to be confused with the suspension *ex informata conscientia*. The Local Ordinary could not suspend them from hearing the confes-

[53] C. 108, § 1.

[54] Cf. CC. 2255, § 2 and 118.

[55] For the extent of the suspension, cf. cc. 2281, 2282.

[56] Tonsure is the ordinary means of incardination,—c. 111; for the other means, cf. cc. 112-117.

[57] C. 94, § 1. Cf. Vermeersch-Creusen, *Epitome*, III, 373.

[58] CC. 874, 619.

[59] *"Potest etiam Episcopus ex informata conscientia suspendere ab audiendis confessionibus regulares, licet a se cum nulla temporis limitatione approbatos, ex nova superveniente causa confessiones concernente, absque eo quod teneatur eam ipsis regularibus significare ut declaravit Clemens X"*—Giraldi, *Expositio Juris Pontificii*, Pars II, sect. 43; Clement X, const. *Superna*, 21 iunii, 1670. *Fontes*, n. 246.

sions of exempt religious, because in this matter, the Local Ordinary has no jurisdiction over them.[60]

Religious Ordinaries can suspend *ex informata conscientia* only the religious subject to them.[61] Religious Ordinaries can likewise suspend their subjects from the use of the faculties granted them by Local Ordinaries; however, in this case, the suspension *ex informata conscientia* would not render the use of the faculties invalid, but only illicit.[62] This has been settled by the Holy See. To the question put in the case, the Sacred Congregation replied affirmatively, *ita tamen ut religiosus suspensus illicite non vero invalide confessiones excipiat.*[63]

Ordinaries can use this suspension *ex informata conscientia* against their subject only *tamquam delinquentes.*[64] It is explicitly stated in canon 2191 that only crimes furnish a basis for this suspension. If the clerics have not been guilty of a crime, and they are not properly fitted to perform their duties, various other means are at the disposal of the Ordinary.

Article IV—Extraordinary Measure

After granting the permission to Ordinaries to proceed with a suspension *ex informata conscientia* in the first paragraph of canon 2186, the legislator, in the second part of the same canon, immediately qualifies the use of this power, and says that it is an extraordinary measure, to be used only when it is impossible to proceed according to the norms of law, without a grave inconvenience.

[60] Benedict XIV, const. *Firmandis,* 6 nov. 1744, § 4; Wernz-Vidal, *Jus Canonicum,* VI, n. 799.

[61] Molitor, *Religiosi Iuris Capita Selecta,* p. 263; Bizarri, *Collectanea,* p. 755; Wernz, *Jus Decretalium,* III, n. 691; Ferraris, verbo *approbatio,* art. 2, n. 20.

[62] Cf. Vermeersch-Creusen, *Epitome,* III, n. 373.

[63] S. C. EE et RR, *Ordinis Praedicatorum,* 2 mart. 1886; Suarez, *De Remotione Parochorum,* p. 216.

[64] Molitor, *Kanonisches Gerichtsverfahren,* p. 225; Hinschius, *Kathol. Kirchenrechts,* V, 610; Bouix, *De Judiciis,* II, 342; Blat, *Commentarium,* IV, 705.

The suspension is called an extraordinary remedy.[65] The word 'remedy' is used loosely, and not in the strict canonical sense of that term;[66] in other parts of this same section this suspension is properly called a *poena*.[67] It is extraordinary—opposed to the ordinary means of procedure. This extraordinary procedure was established by the Council of Trent to counteract extraordinary conditions in the Church; it was to be used only when other means of procedure were unable to safeguard the dignity of the Church from the vices of her ministers.[68] Only when the nature of the case, in view of the circumstances of place and person or the interest of public tranquillity, and the absence of the ordinary means necessitates it, can this extraordinary procedure be used, and it must cease as soon as one can follow the ordinary procedure.[69] In the light of its institution and its historical development, the term extraordinary, as applied to the suspension *ex informata conscientia*, is certainly used as synonymous with the term extrajudicial.

Quia media poenalia spectant ad forum externum, in quo proceditur juxta acta et probata judicialiter convictum, regula generalis est poenas non decerni nisi in reum judicialiter convictum aut confessum; quamobrem sententia condemnatoria ex informata conscientia seu ex morali certitudine judicialiter non comparata, est remedium extraordinarium utpote extrajudiciale.[70]

Whether the same interpretation of the word 'extraordinary' is tenable under Code legislation is questionable.[71] This extraordinary measure is to be used only when the Ordinary cannot proceed according to the norm of law. Does this *ad normam juris* refer only to judicial procedure, or does it refer likewise to the procedure *ad*

[65] *"Dicitur hoc remedium extraordinarium quia justitia postulat ut reus omnibus modis legitimis defendere possit."*—Bouuaert-Simenon, *Manuale*, n. 1233; Bouix, *De Judiciis*, II, 343.

[66] Cf. c. 2306.

[67] CC. 2188, 2°, 2190.

[68] Cf. Wernz-Vidal, *Jus Canonicum*, VI, 759.

[69] Vering, *Droit Canon*, II, 452.

[70] Lega, *De Judiciis Ecclesiasticis*, IV, n. 384; cf. also Conc. Trid. Sess. XIV, cap. 1 de reform.; Benedict XIV, *De Synodo Dioecena*, lib. XII, c. 8, n. 3; Inst. S. C. de P. F.,—*Collectanea*, n. 1628, where this is clearly the meaning of 'extraordinary.'

[71] Cf. Suarez, *De Remotione Parochorum*, p. 220.

modum praecepti? If the first is true, then in Code legislation even as in the older law, the word *extraordinary* is used in opposition only to the term *judicial* and is still therefore synonymous with the term *extrajudicial.* However, if the *ad norman juris* includes the procedure by precept, the word *extraordinary* is used not merely as *extrajudicial,* but more extensively, in opposition both to the judicial mode of procedure and the mode of procedure by precept.

The words ad norman juris evidently comprehend whatever means are instituted by the law to deal with crimes. Therefore the word *extraordinary* as used in canon 2186, § 2 stamps the suspension *ex informata conscientia* as something opposed to the ordinary means provided elsewhere in the law, by which crimes are to be punished *ad norman juris.* Besides the suspension *ex informata conscientia* there are two methods of procedure, judicial procedure, and the extrajudicial procedure *per modum praecepti.* An examination of the canons dealing with the punishment of crimes, leads to the conclusion that both these modes of procedure must be called ordinary modes, and that therefore the suspension *ex informata conscientia* is called an extraordinary remedy in opposition to both, and not, as in the old law, in opposition only to the judicial procedure.[72]

The object of criminal judicial procedure are public crimes.[73] The ordinary procedure in punishing public crimes is therefore the judicial procedure. There are exceptions to this general norm. In the second paragraph of canon 1933 an exception is made for certain crimes, which are to be treated by special penal sanctions.[74] These special penal sanctions are concerned with crimes proper only to clerics. These special penal sanctions therefore are clearly constituted by the legislator as an exception, exempting from judicial procedure certain crimes which are to be punished by definite non-judicial modes of procedure. Besides these exceptions, there is another non-judicial procedure established by law. This is the

[72] This question has been treated thoroughly for the first time by Suarez in his recent book. In discussing it here, the present writer follows to a large extent this treatment by Suarez. Valuable aid on the question was likewise derived from Noval's articles in the *Jus Pontificium,* to which reference will be made.

[73] C. 1933, § 1.

[74] CC. 2168-2194.

procedure by means of precept: "*Poenitentia, remedium poenale, excommunicatio, suspensio, interdictum, dummodo delictum certum sit, infligi possunt etiam per modum praecepti extra judicium.*" [75]

In order to have a clear concept of the exact meaning of canon 2186, § 2 it is necessary to study canon 1933 a little more closely. Does the fourth paragraph of this canon, (establishing the procedure by precept), constitute an exception to the first paragraph of the same canon, (making public crimes the object of judicial procedure)? If it constitutes an exception, then it would follow, that a twofold mode of procedure is possible *ad normam juris* in dealing with public crimes; then the option would be left to the superior either to proceed judicially against the delinquent or to proceed by means of a precept. It is not difficult to see to what consequences such an option would lead.[76]

> *Etenim si superioribus daretur facultas in casibus in § 4 signatis et quando crimina sunt publica, ad procedendum vel judicialiter vel ad modum praecepti, fere numquam judicialiter procederet, cum hoc ipsis onerosius erit, et generaliter loquendo superiores a formis judicialibus abhorreant; sed praecepto semper uterentur, ut via expeditiori. Jam vero nemo non videt inconvenientia ex neglectis formis judicialibus in poenis infligendis adeo gravioribus, ut ex. gr. excommunicatio, ita ut ad ipsam infligendam ne quidem vult Codex judicem unicum, sed praecipit, ut fiat a tribunali trium judicum.*[77]

Even aside from an argument based upon the absurd consequences to which such an interpretation would lead, the text itself is opposed to the theory that paragraph 4 constitutes an exception to paragraph 1: "*Probatur ex c. 1933, § 1: Delicta quae cadunt sub criminali judicio sunt delicta publica. Etenim loco hujus propositionis potest absdubio substitui haec alia quae ex ea necessario consequitur vel potius eidem aequipollet: Delicta publica cadunt sub criminali iudicio.*" [78] In view of this it must be said that public crimes are to be punished regularly by means of criminal judicial

[75] C. 1933, § 4.

[76] Cf. Bouix, *De Judiciis*, II, 343; Wernz-Vidal, *Jus Canonicum*, VI, n. 795.

[77] Suarez, *De Remotione Parochorum*, p. 222.

[78] Noval, "De Ratione Corrigendi,"—*Jus Pont.*, II, (1922), 150. This argument based upon the grammatical construction of the text, and its logical equivalent is developed extensively by Noval in the article cited.

procedure, and that the option is not given to the superior to proceed against such crimes in any other manner.[79] Therefore paragraph 4 of canon 1933, stating that certain penalties may be imposed by precept, does not constitute an exception to paragraph 1, but is concerned with a different mode of procedure for other crimes.[80] The special processes of the third part of the tract on *De Processibus* (2168-2183) are considered ordinary norms of procedure; however since these special processes are concerned with specific crimes, and are not to be extended beyond the crimes specifically mentioned there, no further consideration need be given to that subject here.[81]

The judicial procedure is therefore the ordinary means of procedure in punishing public crimes. All public crimes can be punished by this means of procedure only, with the exception of those which the legislator expressly exempts, namely, crimes against residence,[82] concubinage,[83] pastoral negligence,[84] and those public crimes exempted by reason of canon 2191, § 3. These exceptions are the only positive exceptions legalized by the Code.[85] Beyond these, the only possible exception would be the impossibility of dealing with a public crime in the judicial procedure, whether this impossibility be physical or moral. In the case of physical or moral impossibility of punishing public crimes in judgment, and for all occult crimes the ordinary means of procedure is the procedure *ad modum praecepti.*[86]

Applying these principles concerning the ordinary modes of procedure to the interpretation of canon 2186, § 2, the following conclusions are warranted. The procedure *ex informata conscientia* is an extraordinary mode of procedure—extraordinary in opposition to the two ordinary modes of procedure, the criminal judicial process, and the process by precept—and is to be used only when pro-

79 "*Remedium extraordinarium semper cessare debet dum remedium ordinarium minime defecit*"—Pallottini, *Pugna Juris Pontifii*, p. 98.

80 Cf. Noval, "De Ratione Corrigendi,"—*Jus Pont.*, II (1922), 152.

81 Cf. Blat, *Commentarium,* IV, n. 793; Vermeersch-Creusen, *Epitome,* III, n. 258.

82 CC. 2168-2175.

83 CC. 2176-2181.

84 CC. 2182-2185.

85 Cf. Noval, "De Ratione Corrigendi,"—*Jus Pont.*, II (1922), 152.

86 C. 1933, § 4.

cedure according to the norm of law is impossible. Suspension *ex informata conscientia* deals primarily with occult crimes,[87] and the ordinary procedure in punishing occult crimes is the process by precept; therefore in applying the suspension *ex informata conscientia* in cases of occult crimes, the words *ad normam juris* of 2186, § 2, can refer only to the procedure by precept, since judicial procedure is eliminated in such cases.[88] The ordinary and normal procedure in dealing with public crimes is the criminal judicial process. However, the suspension *ex informata conscientia* can in some cases be applied to public crimes.[89] It has been pointed out above that in the case of physical or moral impossibility, even public crimes could be punished by means of precept. The latter means is an ordinary means of procedure. Therefore, in cases where it is impossible to punish by judicial procedure, the words *ad normam juris* of canon 2186, § 2—in as far as the suspension is concerned with public crimes—refer to both of the ordinary means of procedure. Consequently, a suspension *ex informata conscientia* cannot be imposed for public crimes, even under the circumstances enumerated in canon 2191, § 3, unless it is impossible to proceed without a grave inconvenience, according to the norm of law, i.e., by the judicial procedure, or the procedure by means of precept.[90]

It has been shown that the suspension *ex informata conscientia* is an extraordinary process, opposed to the ordinary processes of punishment.[91] Does it follow then that it must be considered as

[87] C. 2191, § 1.

[88] C. 1933, § 1.

[89] C. 2191, § 3.

[90] Noval summarized these conclusions very briefly: *Extra judicium, sed servato extraordinario processu ex informata conscientia, qui praescribitur et describitur in c. 2186-2194, puniri potest quodlibet delictum clericorum: (a) occultum (2191), si Ordinarius non potest sine gravi incommodo ad juris normam, idest, ad modum praecepti in subditum procedere (2186, § 2), et (b) etiam delictum publicum si versetur in adjunctis expressis in c. 2191, §3, impedientibus eius coercitionem iudicialem, neque alio modo puniri possit sine gravi incommodo ad iuris normam, seu ad modum praecepti.* "De Ratione Corrigendi,"—*Jus Pont.*, III (1923), 38.

[91] "*Processus ex informata conscientia non est iuris norma processualis, hoc sensu quod nequit adhiberi quando servari possunt processus iudicialis, aut ad*

entirely different from the judicial procedure, and the procedure by precept, or is it in some way analogous to either of these processes? It is certainly distinct and entirely different from the judicial procedure. Furthermore it is distinct from the ordinary process by precept, yet at the same time seems to participate in the nature of the latter. Among older canonists and in many decisions of the Sacred Congregation, the suspension *ex information conscientia* is called a precept.[92] The conclusion is warranted therefore that in pre-Code legislation the suspension *ex informata conscientia* was considered a precept. The nature of a precept does not, however, seem to have been so definitely and canonically established as a special process in the pre-Code legislation; therefore an argument from such sources is not entirely conclusive. Although under present legislation, the process by precept is established as a definite canonical procedure,[93] the extent of this procedure is not satisfactorily established by the Code. Thus it is not clear from the Code whether the process by precept is distinct from the precept as a canonical remedy.[94] It seems that it is.[95] But whether this is granted or not, there are indications in the Code pointing strongly to the conclusion that the suspension *ex informata conscientia* is a form of precept. In the legislation concerning the procedure of a suspension by precept, explicit reference is made to the suspension *ex informata conscientia: ". . . Si vero poena latae vel ferendae sententiae inflicta sit ad modum praecepti particularis, scripto aut coram duobus testibus ordinarie declaretur vel irrogetur, indicatis poenae causis salvo praescripto can.* 2193." [96] This would seem to indicate that suspensions *ex informata conscientia* are considered precepts. Again in the canon dealing with the appeal or recourse from censures, reference is made only to those imposed by "a judicial sentence or

modum praecepti, sed est iuris norma extraordinaria."—Noval, "De Ratione Corrigendi,"—*Jus Pont.*, III (1923), 38.

[92] Cf. Instr. S. C. de P. F., n. 2, 3,—*Collectanea*, N. 1628; S. C. EE. et RR., *Ordinis Praedicatorum*, 2 mart. 1886.

[93] C. 1933, § 4.

[94] C. 2306.

[95] Cf. Suarez, *De Remotione Parochorum*, p. 226.

[96] C. 2225.

by means of precept."[97] From these considerations, it is inferred that the suspension *ex informata conscientia* is imposed by means of a precept, but of a precept of its own peculiar nature.[98]

This extraordinary means of punishment can be used only when the Ordinary cannot proceed according to the norms of law without a grave inconvenience. "This procedure should be employed only by ways of an exception, rarely and moderately, only when the good of souls imperiously requires the repression of an occult crime. One must not forget that human authority does not have to punish all crimes, according to the well-known adage: *Si omnia in hoc saeculo vindicanda essent, locum divina judicia non habent.*"[99] Just what constitutes a grave inconvenience is not mentioned. It is certain, however, that the inconvenience must be truly grave in proportion to the nature of the suspension itself.[100] Although the final judgment as to what constitutes a grave inconvenience rests with the Ordinary,[101] he must be governed by sound reason, and not by exaggerated opinions.[102] In case of inflicting this suspension for public crimes, the circumstances enumerated in canon 2191, § 3 constitute a grave inconvenience,[103] but it must not be overlooked that the words *sine gravi incommodo* apply to both the judicial process and the process by precept.[104] As illustrations of circumstances constituting a grave inconvenience, authors cite the following: Great difficulty or impossibility of avoiding a grave public scandal in the ordinary procedure; probable danger lest the guilty person, to the great detriment of the sacred ministry, cannot be removed from office; serious harm resultant to witnesses, should their names be revealed;

[97] C. 2243, § 1.

[98] Cf. Suarez, *De Remotione Parochorum*, p. 226.

[99] Vering, *Droit Canon*, II, 446.

[100] Cf. Bouix, *De Judiciis*, II, 345.

[101] "As supreme administrator, it is for the Bishop to determine the fitness of employing an extrajudicial procedure; . . . but . . . he must take the responsibility of his actions." Peries, "Suspension ex Informata Conscientia"—*ER*, XV (1896), 202.

[102] ". . . *quatenus gravissimas et canonicas causas concurrere in Domino judicaverint* . . ."—Inst., 20 iul. 1878—Smith, *Elements of Ecclesiastical Law*, II, n. 1307.

[103] Cf. Suarez, *De Remotione Parochorum*, p. 226.

[104] Cf. Noval, "De Ratione Corrigendi"—*Jus Pont.*, III (1923), 38.

probable danger of the civil law impeding the jurisdiction of the ecclesiastical court; danger that the Ordinary may be sued for defamation in a civil law suit, and similar causes.[105] If it is clearly evident that no grave inconvenience exists, the suspension *ex informata conscientia* would be invalid, since it would be an act beyond the jurisdiction of the Ordinary. This is an extraordinary power granted under qualifications, and must be interpreted strictly as an aberration from the ordinary norm of law. However the suspension can be said to be invalid only when it is clearly *evident* that the Ordinary could proceed otherwise without a grave inconvenience.[106] If the matter is doubtful, since it is left to the prudence of the Ordinary to determine the sufficient gravity of the inconvenience, the suspension would certainly have to be considered valid, but recourse may be had to the Holy See.

[105] Cf. Vermeersch-Creusen, *Epitome*, III, n. 373. "*Maxime vero nostra aetate cum processus criminalis contra clericos in Codice sit ordinata cum maiori claritate et simplicitate, ita ut non multum differat a processu summario iuris praecedentis, qui tempore Conc. Tridentini nondum erat introductus et pro pluribus casibus praesto adsit unus ex processibus administrativis seu disciplinaribus, de quibus can. 2142 seq., frequentius iam adhiberi poterit processus criminalis vel disciplinaris, neque tam frequenter occurret necessitas unice procedendi ex informata conscientia.*" Wernz-Vidal, *Jus Canonicum*, VI, n. 795.

[106] Even in this case, Bouix maintains that the suspension would be valid although illicit. He states however that in such a case the Sacred Congregation would rescind the decree of the Ordinary. Cf. Bouix, *De Judiciis*, II, 346.

CHAPTER V

CAUSES FOR WHICH THE SUSPENSION *EX INFORMATA CONSCIENTIA* CAN BE IMPOSED

Canon 2191. §1. Suspensioni ex informata conscientia iustam ac legitimam causam praebet delictum occultum ad normam can. 2197, n. 4.

§ 2. Ob notorium delictum suspensio ex informata conscientia nunquam ferri potest.

§ 3. Ut delictum publicum suspensione ex informata conscientia plecti possit, occurrat necesse est aliquod ex adiunctis quae sequuntur:

1°. Si testes probi et graves delictum quidem Ordinario patefaciant, sed nulla ratione induci possint ut de eo testimonium in iudicio ferant, neque aliis probationibus delictum iudiciali processu evinci possit;

2°. Si ipsemet clericus minis aut aliis adhibitis mediis impediat ne processus iudiciarius instituatur aut inceptus perficiatur;

3°. Si processui iudiciali conficiendo ferendaeque sententiae impedimenta exoriantur ex adversis civilibus legibus aut gravi scandali periculo.

In this canon are numerated the causes for which this suspension can be applied. In the first place it may be imposed for an occult crime. Secondly, it may never be imposed for a notorious crime. Thirdly, it may be imposed for certain public crimes. Per se, this suspension is for occult crimes, but if the circumstances enumerated in the canon are present in the case of a public crime, this extraordinary measure may be used.

Article I—Nature and Classification of Crime

Since a crime *(delictum)* and only a crime, can be the cause on account of which this suspension *ex informata conscientia* can be imposed, it is necessary for the proper understanding of the use of this extraordinary measure to have a clear concept of the exact meaning of a 'crime'. There is question here of an extraordinary measure and consequently one which must be at all times interpreted strictly. For this reason, the word 'crime' cannot be taken in any but its strictly legal sense. Many things are called crimes: in the moral order, ordinarily the more grievous sins are classified as crimes; then too in the civil order, the word 'crime' applies to a definite class of legal offenses, offenses which are of a more serious nature. The suspension *ex informata conscientia* is a purely ecclesiastical means of procedure, and deals only with ecclesiastical 'crimes'.

By a crime, in ecclesiastical law, is meant an external and morally imputable violation of a law to which there is attached a canonical sanction, at least an indeterminate one.[1] This is the definition of a crime in its strictly ecclesiastical sense. However, participating in the nature of a crime, and considered as equivalent as far as legal consequences are concerned, are the violations of precepts which have penal sanctions.[2] In this connection it is evident that the only precept which is under consideration is the precept issued in view of the power of jurisdiction. A precept is a command or prohibition given by a superior to an inferior, and may be issued either by virtue of the power of jurisdiction, or by virtue of dominative authority. Since only those who have the power of jurisdiction, can impose ecclesiastical penalties, the precept to which a canonical sanction can be attached is only the precept which is given in virtue or the power of jurisdiction and not the precept given by virtue of dominative authority.[3] In view of the definition which has been given of a crime in the ecclesiastical sense, its differentiation from 'sin' is evident.[4] *"Quod considerare oportet est quod ad constituendum delictum, quod est ens juridicum, non sufficit merum peccatum, quod est ens morale."* [5]

A crime therefore is an external violation of a penal law. Ex-

[1] C. 2195, § 1.

[2] C. 2195, § 2.

[3] Vermeersch-Creusen, *Epitome*, III, n. 383.

[4] Cf. Ayrinhac, *Penal Legislation*, p. 26; Vermeersch-Creusen, *Epitome*, III, n. 383.

[5] Suarez, *De Remotione Parochorum*, p. 247.

ternal is used here in contradistinction to internal, and signifies an act which is so performed as to be able to be perceived by some external sense; note, that the possibility to be perceived is the determining factor, and not the actual perception. As long therefore as an act remains purely internal, no matter how grievous a sin it may be, e.g., hatred, unbelief, etc., it is not a crime, and therefore not subject to punishment in the external forum.

Further, the external violation must be morally imputable.[6] In this sense, every crime is likewise a sin, while contrariwise every sin is not a crime. The imputability of an external violation is derived from one of two sources, *dolus* or *culpa*.[7] *Dolus* is the deliberate will of violating the law,[8] while *culpa* consists in the ignorance of the law which is violated, or in the omission of due diligence;[9] the latter at times approximates *dolus*.[10] All the causes which operate to increase, lessen or destroy either *dolus* or *culpa*, by that very fact likewise increase, lessen or destroy the imputability of the crime.[11]

The external, morally imputable violation must furthermore be concerned with definite laws, namely, laws to which is attached a canonical sanction, in order that it constitute a crime.[12] A sanction is a penalty imposed by ecclesiastical law for the violation of its law. The penalty or sanction can be either determinate or indeterminate. It is determinate if in the law itself or precept, it is *taxative* decreed; it is indeterminate if the infliction of the penalty is left to the judgment of the judge or superior, whether preceptively or facultatively.[13] An indeterminate sanction is sufficient to constitute an external morally imputable violation a crime. It is sometimes difficult to determine whether a law is sanctioned even indeterminately. This special difficulty arises particularly in the case of grave scandal, or

[6] "The moral guilt, however, frequently is and has to be presumed *in foro externo*." Ayrinhac, *Penal Legislation*, p. 26.

[7] C. 2199.

[8] C. 2200.

[9] C. 2199.

[10] C. 2203.

[11] C. 2199.

[12] Cf. Ayrinhac, *Penal Legislation*, 27.

[13] C. 2217, n. 1.

of the special gravity of the transgression of a law, to which no sanction is attached.

"Licet lex nullam sanctionem appositam habeat, legitimus tamen superior potest illius transgressionem etiam sine praevia poenae comminatione, aliqua justa poena punire, si scandalum forte datum aut specialis transgressionis gravitas id ferat; secus reus puniri nequit nisi prius monitus fuerit cum comminatione poenae latae vel ferendae sententiae in casu transgressionis, et nihilominus legem violaverit." [14]

Does the gravity of the scandal, or the special gravity of the transgression, in these cases render the violation of the law a crime? *Prima facie,* it would not seem so, in view of the wording of the canon itself, *licet lex nullam sanctionem appositam habeat.* This seems evidently opposed to the idea that what follows should constitute a sanction. However, a closer study of the nature of this canon, renders the question at least doubtful, with the preponderance of probability in favor of the view that in this canon, there is truly a question of an indeterminate sanction.[15] Here the superior is given permission to impose a penalty, even without previous warning, for the violation of a law, to which no sanction is expressly attached—if the circumstances of grave scandal or of special gravity are present. This permission to punish certainly seems to be an indeterminate sanction, made to cover general cases where the special circumstances are present.[16] Consequently such transgressions must be considered crimes, and considered as coming within the scope of the cause of the suspension *ex informata conscientia.*

Elementum legale delicti non deest, cum lex communis illo canone contenta auctoritatem tribuat puniendi ideoque vera sit lex poenalis, comminans sanctionem indeterminatam et arbitrio illius Superioris determinandam, cui commissum est prudens iudicium de verificata causa scandali aut de legis gravitate ex generalibus iuris principiis et ex specialibus loci cirumstantiis aestimanda.[17]

Previous to the Code, authors found it quite a difficult matter

[14] C. 2222, § 1.

[15] The addition of an indeterminate sanction to a law made be made *"a) in ipso momento conditionis legis, . . .; b) vel postea, . . .; c) vel antea, id est, vi can. 2222, si scandalum forte datum aut specialis transgressionis gravitas id ferat, necnon c.* 2229 § 4."—Noval, *De Processibus,* n. 751.

[16] Cf. Vermeersch-Creusen, *Epitome,* III, n. 383.

[17] Vidal, "Notio Delicti in iure Codicis,"—*Jus Pont.,* I (1921), 101.

to determine the proper classification and line of demarcation of public and occult crimes.[18] It has been stated earlier in this work that this was a question of special difficulty in regard to the application of the suspension *ex informata conscientia.*[19] Now however there remains little difficulty since the Code has given a very clear and distinct classification.[20]

A crime is public if it has been already divulged, or if it is in such circumstances that it can be prudently judged that the crime can and must be easily divulged.[21] The Code here gives the definition of 'public' in its application to a crime, and classifies two cases under this appellation, actual publicity and virtual publicity. A crime is public actually, if the crime itself and the author of the crime are known generally; with regard to the imputability, it is not necessary that this be known with absolute certainty, otherwise there would be no distinction between a public and a notorious crime; on the other hand there must be some evidence of the imputability, otherwise there would be no distinction between public and occult crimes. A crime is public virtually if it can be prudently judged that it soon will be actually public; thus if loquacious persons know of it, or if there are other circumstances strongly tending to its further revelation, the crime would be virtually public. The Code does not specify how far the crime must be divulged to constitute publicity; however certainly if it is known to the major portion of a community, or if the persons knowing of it will probably inform the greater portion of the community, such knowledge would constitute publicity.[22]

A crime may be notorious either by notoriety of fact or by

[18] Some canonists allowed the Ordinary discretion in determining whether the crime was public or occult. Cf. Lucidi, *De Visitatione SS.LL.*, I, n. 272; Smith, *Elements of Ecclesiastical Law,* II, n. 1309.

[19] Cf. The first part of this work, pp. 24-33.

[20] Cf. Vermeersch-Creusen, *Epitome,* III, n. 379.

[21] C. 2197, 1°.

[22] Cf. Vermeersch-Creusen, *Epitome,* III, n. 379; Ayrinhac, *Penal Legislation,* p. 29; Bouuaert-Simenon, *Manuale,* n. 1241. Authors ordinarily give as a norm in this matter numbers relative to the size of the community. In a very small community, two or three persons knowing of the crime, may constitute sufficient publicity.

notoriety of law. It may be notorious by notoriety of law in two ways:

(a) After the sentence of a competent judge which has become a closed matter *(res judicata)*.[23] A sentence becomes a *res judicata* in various ways: a twofold conformable sentence, a sentence to which an appeal is not taken within the time *(tempus utile)* granted for such an appeal, or by a definitive sentence to which no appeal is possible.[24] The legal effect of this transition of a sentence to a *res judicata* is a *presumptio juris et de jure* that the sentence is true and just and consequently cannot be directly attacked.[25]

(b) After a judicial confession of the guilty party.[26] A judicial confession is the written or oral admission of guilt against oneself by the guilty party in the presence of the judge, whether spontaneously given or upon interrogation by the judge.[27]

A crime is notorious by notoriety of fact, if it is publicly known and if it was committed in such circumstances that it can be concealed by no subterfuge, nor excused by any interpretation of law.[28] There are two conditions necessary, publicity as to the fact, and certainty as to the imputability of the crime; it is evident that such a case will rarely exist; there are so many things which may influence the imputability of a crime, and so many circumstances to be taken into consideration, that prudence will dictate a very cautious procedure in calling a crime notorious by notoriety of fact.[29] Thus, e.g., homicide committed before a large number of people would seem to be a notorious fact; however unless the criminal intent was evident, (no excuse of self-defense or any justification) the crime would not be notorious.[30]

A crime is occult if it is not public; materially occult if the crime

[23] C. 2197, 2°.

[24] C. 1902.

[25] C. 1904, § 1.

[26] C. 2197, 2°.

[27] C. 1750.

[28] C. 2197, 3°.

[29] Cf. Noval, *De Processibus*, n. 757; Suarez, *De Remotione Parochorum*, 250; Bouuaert-Simenon, *Manuale*, n. 1241.

[30] Cf. Ayrinhac, *Penal Legislation*, p. 30; Ferreres, *Institutiones Canonicae*, II, n. 948.

itself is not known; formally occult if its imputability is not known.[31] The Code thus defines an occult crime negatively. If the crime itself is known only to a few persons, who will not divulge it, or if its imputability is known only to a few, it is occult. The quality of the persons knowing of the crime, rather than the number is the determining factor, in the distinction between public and occult. The number further must be reckoned in proportion to the size of the community.

Article II—Causes of the Suspension

The suspension *ex informata conscientia* can be inflicted only for crimes,[32] and these crimes must be sufficiently grave as to merit such a grave punishment.[33] As examples of such crimes a few may be mentioned; repeated sins against the sixth commandment, more particularly qualified sins committed with another person; frequent and serious excess in the use of intoxicating drinks; qualified sins of the seventh commandment, especially if of a very grave amount; in general, those crimes which, according to the Code, can be or are punished by reserved excommunication or other reserved penalties.[34] However this extraordinary measure is not to be used to punish all grave crimes, even though their gravity is such as to require ecclesiastical penalties.[35] It is primarily to be used as a method of procedure in the case of occult crimes, whether materially or formally occult, and in these cases only when it is impossible to proceed according to the ordinary procedure in such cases, namely, the procedure by precept. Occult crimes are to be interpreted strictly, and only such considered as fall within the Code definition of occult, and not the

[31] C. 2197, 4°.

[32] *"Si agatur de poena suspensionis a divinis (vel ab officio), haec perfecto non est herba Betonica in omnibus emplastris adhibenda, prout nonnulli Ordinarii opinantur, qui in omnibus casibus et pro quacumque causa censuris abutuntur eosque, licet maximopere formidandis, propter frequentem usum seu verius abusum reddunt contemptiles, sed nonnisi ob culpam lethalem Ordinariis illam comminari seu fulminaee potest."*—Benedict XIV, *De Synodo Dioecesana. Lib.* XII, c. 1, n. 35.

[33] C. 2190.

[34] Cf. Vermeersch-Creusen, *Epitome,* III, n. 381.

[35] Cf. Vering, *Droit Canon,* II, 448.

many really public crimes which authors formerly, by means of interpretation, read into the meaning of occult.[36]

In the second paragraph of canon 2191 it is expressly stated that the suspension *ex informata conscientia* can not be used to punish notorious crimes. The suspension *ex informata conscientia* is to be used only when other measures are unavailable, and in the case of notorious crimes, much simpler measures of procedure are available and there is no need to resort to this extraordinary measure.[37] It might be urged that the special circumstances under which public crimes may be punished by suspension *ex informata conscientia* demand that this same extraordinary procedure be allowed under the same circumstances in the case of notorious crimes. This is fallacious.[38] The first circumstance is the refusal of witnesses to testify, but in notorious crimes, the testimony of witnesses is not needed for proof, because notorious facts need no proof.[39] The second circumstance is the impediment placed by the guilty person to the judicial process; but for notorious crimes the judicial process is not necessary because the judicial procedure is for public crimes.[40] The third circumstance is the opposition of civil law, but this is based mainly on the fear of suit for defamation against the Bishop in a civil court, and this is unlikely where the crime is notorious, because defamation cannot then be easily adduced. For these reasons, the Code prohibits the use of the suspension *ex informata conscientia* to punish notorious crimes, and its use for this purpose is absolutely invalid,[41] because the wording of the law is clearly invalidating "*ferri nunquam potest.*"

The suspension *ex informata conscientia* cannot be used to punish public crimes, unless one of the circumstances, mentioned *taxative* in paragraph 3, is present. In the historical review of this question, it has been shown that the traditional interpretation limited the

[36] "*Cavere tamen quisque debet episcopus, ne, quod publicum et notorium jam est, perinde ac esset occultum, falso sibi animo reputans, suspensionem ex informata conscientia decernat.*"—Lucidi, *De Visitatione SS.LL.*, I, n. 272.

[37] Cf. Noval, *De Processibus*, n. 444.

[38] Cf. Vermeersch-Creusen, *Epitome*, III, n. 379.

[39] C. 1747, 1°.

[40] C. 1933, § 1.

[41] Cf. Arndt, "Die Suspension,"—*AKKR*, 73 (1895), 154.

suspension *ex informata conscientia* to occult crimes.[42] In general it can be said that the traditional interpretation was correct, meaning that the suspension *ex informata conscientia* is primarily for occult crimes. Numerous decisions, quoted in the first part of this work, clearly indicate the historical interpretation of the decree of the Council of Trent. However, it was conceded that under certain circumstances the suspension *ex informata conscientia* was almost necessary to punish certain public crimes. This difficulty was circumvented by defining 'occult' in a sense broad enough to include such cases. The definition offered by Santi is fairly representative of this trend of thought. Santi calls that crime occult which cannot be proved in a judicial trial, or even though proofs could be presented in a trial, yet it cannot be done without a grave danger of scandal to the faithful, or a serious damage to the cleric.[43] On the other hand there were some canonists who maintained that the Tridentine suspension *ex informata conscientia* should be so interpreted as to include public crimes in certain well defined cases.[44] The Instruction of Sacred Congregation of 1884 however explicitly limited the suspension *ex informata conscientia* to occult crimes.[45] The Code, while limiting it to occult crimes, admits its use for public crimes under certain well defined circumstances.[46] Public crimes are ordinarily to be punished through means of the judicial procedure, precisely established for this purpose;[47] if then an ordinary judicial procedure

[42] Cf. Smith, *Elements of Ecclesiastical Law,* II, n. 1294.

[43] Santi-Leitner, *Praelectiones Juris Ecclesiasticae,* V, n. 18; similar definitions are offered by Wernz, *Jus Decretalium,* V, n. 41; Droste-Messmer, *Canonical Procedure,* p. 158; *Analecta Juris Pontificii,* XIX, 1228; Hergenroether, *Kathol. Kirchenrecht,* p. 364. Tendencies to such a wide interpretation are still discernible in a few modern canonists; cf. Suarez, *De Remotione Parochorum,* p. 252; Vermeersch-Creusen, *Epitome,* III, n. 379; Bouuaert-Simenon, *Manuale,* n. 1235.

[44] Cf. Bouix, *De Judiciis,* II, 325; Peries, "Suspension ex Informata Conscientia,"—*ER,* XV (1896), 249.

[45] *Collectanea,* n. 1628.

[46] "The Code returns to the discipline of the Council of Trent, changing the law of the S. C. de P. F. For the Council of Trent taught that this penalty could be inflicted *etiam ob occultum crimen,*"—Vermeersch-Creusen, *Epitome,* III, n. 379.

[47] Cf. Noval, *De Processibus,* n. 751.

can be followed, that is the means to be used. Recourse to this extraordinary procedure of suspension *ex informata conscientia* is to be had only when the other procedure is impossible, and at the same time it is necessary that the crime be punished.[48] "To admit that public crimes are ordinarily punishable by suspension *ex informata conscientia* would be to undermine the whole judicial and disciplinary system of the Church." [49]

Even before the Code authors admitted that under certain circumstances it was morally, sometimes physically, impossible to follow the ordinary procedure of a judicial process. In these cases they admitted the use of the suspension *ex informata conscientia.* All the circumstances, which are recognized by the Code as justifying the suspension *ex informata conscientia* in the case of public crimes, were recognized by authors as being sufficient ground for the use of the suspension *ex informata conscientia;* however, the authors then maintained that these circumstances render the crime occult, due to the impossibility of proof in a judicial procedure.[50] Such circumstances may still exist, and for this reason the Code has definitely taken them into consideration, and specifies that if any be present, a superior may use the suspension *ex informata conscientia* to punish a public crime.

The first exceptional case is the refusal of witnesses to testify in court: prudent and trustworthy witnesses reveal a crime to the Ordinary, but cannot be induced in any way to testify concerning it in court, and the crime cannot be established in a judicial process by other proofs. In this case, therefore, when there are trustworthy witnesses, whose testimony sufficiently proves a public crime, even though they will not give testimony judicially for any reason whatever, the ordinary may proceed with a suspension *ex informata conscientia.* This is not exactly new legislation. In the past, however, when the witnesses could not be induced to testify in a judicial process and when there were no other proofs, the crime was considered occult, and the suspension *ex informata conscientia* was ad-

[48] Cf. Vering, *Droit Canon,* II, 452.

[49] Peries, "Suspension ex Informata Conscientia,"—*ER,* XV, (1896), 242.

[50] Cf. Droste-Messmer, *Canonical Procedure,* p. 158; Heiner, *Katholisches Kirchenrecht,* II, 43.

mitted. After 1880, however, a distinction was made between the case where the witnesses refused to reveal the crime to the Ordinary, and the case where they were willing to testify to the Ordinary extrajudicially, with the condition that their names be kept silent.[51] In the first case, the suspension could be inflicted, if the Ordinary had certain knowledge from other sources. However, in the latter case the suspension could not be used, because the economic process, established by the Instruction of 1880, could be used.[52] The Code is cautious in granting the right to the Ordinary to proceed in this case, and demands that the testimony only of *testes probi et graves* is to be considered; the Ordinary must have certain knowledge before acting, and this certain knowledge evidently cannot be derived from the testimony of untrustworthy witnesses.[53] That these circumstances can be present is not difficult to understand; a case may easily arise in which trustworthy witnesses may not wish to testify in court, whether from fear of reprisal from the person against whom they testify, or from fear of personal defamation, e.g., in the case of a person testifying who was partner to the crime of which the cleric is accused.[54] The refusal of witnesses to testify constitutes a circumstance allowing the use of the suspension *ex informata conscientia* only when it is coupled with the inadequacy of other proofs; if sufficient testimony can be acquired by other means which will prove the case sufficiently to give the judge moral certitude *ex actis et probatis*,[55] it is evident that the judicial procedure must be followed, and that a suspension *ex informata conscientia* could not be inflicted in such circumstances.[56] On the other hand too there may be circumstances which would not allow the witnesses to testify,[57] and if such circumstances are present coupled with the inadequacy of other

[51] Cf. Lega, *De Judiciis Ecclesiasticis,* IV, n. 395; Suarez, *De Remotione Parochorum,* p. 253.

[52] Instr. S. C. EE et RR, 11 iun. 1880—*Fontes,* n. 2005.

[53] Cf. c. 1791 concerning the juridical value of testimony.

[54] Cf. Suarez, *De Remotione Parochorum,* p. 253.

[55] C. 1869.

[56] Cf. Blat, *Commentarium,* IV, n. 798.

[57] Cf. 1755, § 2 where the causes enumerated certainly establish reasonable cause to induce the witnesses to refuse to testify.

proofs, certainly the Ordinary would be justified in inflicting a suspension *ex informata conscientia.*

The second exceptional case occurs when the guilty cleric impedes the judicial process. If the cleric himself by threats or other means, e.g., by stirring up seditions among the people, or having recourse to the civil power to prohibit an ecclesiastic judicial procedure,[58] or any means whatever, hinders the judicial process from being started, or from continuing, the Ordinary is allowed to inflict a suspension *ex informata conscientia.* This case will not be of such frequent occurrence, but may nevertheless happen. History demonstrates that it has taken place.[59] It is proper that there should be a means of punishing those who thus impede the process of justice from striking them, and the suspension *ex informata conscientia* is the means offered for this purpose. Although the Code simply mentions the case where the progress of justice is impeded by the guilty cleric, it seems that the suspension *ex informata conscientia* could likewise be used in the case when not the cleric himself, but his friends take means to prevent the trial of the cleric; at least if they do this with the connivance and encouragement of the cleric himself; if the cleric, upon the admonition of the Ordinary, makes no effort to remove the obstructions which are being placed to the orderly progress of justice, he is presumed to be favoring these means.[60] However, it is well to note that the Ordinary should be certain that the cleric is impeding the judicial process, before this extreme remedy is invoked.

The third exceptional case embraces two circumstances, either adverse civil laws or fear of a grave scandal. If impediments hindering a judicial process arise from adverse civil law or from the grave danger of scandal, the suspension *ex informata conscientia* may be used. The Code for the first time embodies this case into the legislation of the suspension *ex informata conscientia;* however the substance of it was already held by authors, based on the decisions of the Sacred Congregation. The possibility of the case is not to be minimized, at least in certain countries. In a country where the

[58] Cf. Blat, *Commentarium*, IV, n. 798.

[59] Cf. Suarez, *De Remotione Parochorum*, 253; *Il Monitore Ecclesiastico*, (1921), 368.

[60] Cf. Wernz-Vidal, *Jus Canonicum*, VI, n. 603.

state does not recognize the judiciary and coercive power of the Church, and consequently looks askance at a process instituted by the Church to punish anybody, a delinquent priest, who has been so punished, or who is to be so punished, could cause serious difficulty to the ecclesiastical authorities, either by bringing a suit for libel against his Ordinary, or by obtaining an injunction from a civil court. An example of this third circumstance is cited by authors. A suspension *ex informata conscientia* imposed by the Bishops of Italy on priests subscribing to the letters of Passaglia against the temporal sovereignity of the Pope, was upheld by the Holy See even though the crime was public and was known throughout the kingdom.[61] The Bishops fearing that they would lay themselves open to civil procedure against them if they admitted the cause of the suspension, as would necessarily have to be done in a judicial process, made use of the suspension *ex informata conscientia* to punish the guilty priests.

This difficulty is not of serious importance in the United States, where there is a complete separation of Church and State. Since the administration of ecclesiastical penalties—and certainly the suspension *ex informata conscientia* is only an ecclesiastical penalty—is a matter of ecclesiastical policy, and not of State control, the right of the ecclesiastical court in this country would not be questioned. In fact, according to the trend of legal decisions, it is highly improbable that a civil court would even care to review such a case, much less to interfere in such matters. A decision of the Supreme Court of the United States recognized the decisions of ecclesiastical courts as final in questions of ecclesiastical matters.[62] However even in this country, if the charge of defamation is liable to be brought against the Ordinary in a civil court, the Ordinary could certainly make use of the suspension *ex informata conscientia.* Whether in any particular case, there may be danger that the suspended cleric will resort to a civil suit for defamation, must be prudently judged by the Ordinary, who should take into consideration the character of the cleric, who is to be suspended.

[61] Cf. Cavagnis, *Institutiones Juris Publici,* II, 43; Ferreres, *Institutiones Canonicae,* II, n. 938; the case is given more fully in the first part of this work.

[62] Cf. Watson vs. Jones, 80 U. S. 679.

The other circumstance enumerated in the third exceptional case, is grave fear of scandal. This may occur if from a judicial process greater evils are expected, e.g., if more serious crimes should become known, or those crimes should be made more public, or if a priest's condemnation would cause a serious reaction of the people. Thus if a priest, who is held in high reputation by the majority of his people who do not believe the charges made against him, would be brought to a judicial procedure, grave scandal may result, which will be detrimental to the common good.[63] In this case the supreme law of the *salus animarum* takes precedence, and the Ordinary should proceed with a suspension *ex informata conscientia* quietly, and without allowing the case to become known.

Article III—Special Cases

The causes for which a suspension *ex informata conscientia* may be inflicted have been stated rather thoroughly. It has been shown that the primary cause is occult crime, and that only under special circumstances do public crimes come into consideration. Although the Code is very clear and concise, yet there is a possibility that certain cases may arise which at first sight cannot be clearly catagorized; in order to solve such cases, it is necessary to apply to them the general principles set forth in the preceding articles. A few of the more likely cases, which may offer difficulty, are therefore appended here and briefly considered.

1.

A crime occult at the time when the suspension *ex informata conscientia* is inflicted may later become public. In this case, does the suspension become null by the subsequent publicity of the crime, because suspensions *ex informata conscientia* are inflicted only for occult crimes? The answer must certainly be negative.[64] The suspension is imposed either as a censure and in this case it can be removed only by absolution,[65] or as a vindictive penalty, which can

[63] Cf. Suarez, *De Remotione Parochorum,* p. 254.

[64] Cf. Bassibey, "Des Sentences Ex Informata Conscientia"—*JJC,* II (1893), 340.

[65] C. 2248, § 1.

be ended only by expiation or dispensation.[66] Therefore in either case, the subsequent publicity of a crime, punished by a valid suspension *ex informata conscientia,* does not effect the suspension.

2.

If a person has been absolved in a judicial process, can the Ordinary impose a suspension *ex informata conscientia* for the crime of which he was absolved, provided the Ordinary has certain knowledge of the crime? Before the Code, authors answered the question in the affirmative giving the Bishop power to impose a suspension *ex informata conscientia* in such a case, because if a crime could not be proved by judicial process it was considered occult.[67] Even those authors who were inclined to a very strict interpretation throughout their treatment of the suspension *ex informata conscientia,* on this particular point held the more liberal view. Some, however, distinguish the case before and after acquittal; before and during the trial, the crime is public and cannot be punished by this means; by acquittal the crime becomes occult and consequently there is place for the suspension *ex informata conscientia.*[68]

However, in view of the present Code law, a negative answer seems proper, denying this power to the Ordinary.[69] If the crime in question is public (and this is the assumption, since occult crimes have no place in a judicial process) [70] it is to be punished by a judicial process unless one of the three exceptional circumstances of c. 2191, § 3 is present. If, however, an absolutory sentence is pronounced in favor of a guilty person because one of these three circumstances is present, e.g., because grave and trustworthy witnesses refused to testify in court, then of course there is room for

[66] C. 2289.

[67] Cf. S. C. C., *Perusina,* 26 sept. 1795—*Thesaurus Resolutionum,* LXIV, 196; Pallottini, *Collectio . . . Resolutionum* S. C. C., XVI, n. 167; Wernz, *Jus Decretalium,* V, n. 902; et alii.

[68] Cf. Droste-Messmer, *Canonical Procedure,* p. 159.

[69] Suarez disagrees and bases his argument on the definition of occult and asserts that in the case, the crime, although materially public, would be formally occult. Cf. *De Remotione Parochorum,* p. 255.

[70] C. 1933, § 1.

the suspension *ex informata conscientia.*[71] But if the evidence brought in the case convinces the Ordinary of the guilt of the accused cleric, while it does not convince the judge or judges as the case may be, the Ordinary has no right to use a suspension *ex informata conscientia.*[72] The case may be appealed to a higher Tribunal by the Promotor Justitiae, but pending appeal the accused person is to be considered innocent. Even Suarez, who maintains the opposite position on this question, issues a warning to proceed with the utmost caution:

> *Et eo cautius in hoc remedio utendo in talibus circumstantiis procedi debet quo magis et facilius quis decipitur dum proceditur in negotio jam antea cognito et haudquaquam nobis favorabiliter soluto; sicut in casu praesumendum est Ordinarium maluisse rei condemnationem iudicialem antca actam quam absolutionem eo ipso quod reum agnovit culpabilem.*[73]

3.

Another interesting question—has the Ordinary the right to use a suspension *ex informata conscientia,* while an appeal is pending—was considered in a case settled by the Holy See.[74] In the case, the Diocesan Consistory through a judicial process had suspended a certain priest; the latter appealed the case to the metropolitan court. Pending the appeal, the Bishop suspended him *ex informata conscientia.* Recourse was had to the Holy See and the suspension *ex informata conscientia* was not upheld. Following this decision, authors commonly held that pending an appeal from a condemnatory sentence of the court of the first instance, the Bishop could not suspend such a cleric *ex informata conscientia* without awaiting the outcome of the appeal. Previous to the Code, this was commonly held. Is the opinion still to be maintained? Most assuredly. The principal argument is based on the nature of the suspension *ex informata conscientia* as an extraordinary remedy, to be applied to

[71] Cf. Bassibey, "Des Sentences ex Informata Conscientia"—*JJC,* II, (1893), 340. But even when the Ordinary possesses sufficient extrajudicial testimony to justify his action, Bassibey advises caution in the use of this extreme remedy.

[72] Cf. Heiner, *Katholisches Kirchenrecht,* II, 44.

[73] *De Remotione Parochorum,* p. 256.

[74] Cf. S. C. C., *Bosnien. et Sirmien.,* 20 dec. 1873—*ASS,* VII, 572.

public crimes only when one of the conditions mentioned in canon 2191, § 3 is verified. The supposition is that a cleric has been condemned by a judicial process for a public crime; it must have been a public crime, because occult crimes do not constitute the proper matter for judicial processes; furthermore the suspension *ex informata conscientia* can be applied to public crimes only when the judicial process is not possible; but in the case under consideration, the judicial process had actually taken place. Consequently the Ordinary could not make use of the suspension *ex informata conscientia* against such a cleric for a crime, because of which he had already been condemned, and had used his right to appeal to a higher court.

The second argument and the one which was actually used in attacking the *suspension ex informata conscientia* in the case mentioned [75] is that a suspension is an *attentatum: "Unde consequitur decretum ex informata conscientia tamquam attentatum contra judicem ad quem patet appellatio, mole sua ruere."* [76] This argument is sound. An *attentatum* is anything which, while the case is pending, either party innovates against the other—or the judge against either party or against both—to the prejudice of the party, who does not consent.[77] In the case under consideration, the case is still pending; an appeal *in suspensivo* suspends the execution of the appealéd sentence, and the principle obtains, *lite pendente nihil innovetur;* an appeal *in devolutivo* does not suspend the execution of the appealed sentence, although the case is considered still pending on the merit of the cause;[78] consequently it matters not whether the suspension under consideration was a censure or vindictive penalty. The fact that the sentence was passed by the Consistory and not by the Bishop himself is not vital, because the *officialis* constitutes one tribunal with the Ordinary.[79] A suspension *ex informata conscientia* is certainly prejudicial to the appellant, and such a procedure is truly an *attentatum,* and therefore the suspension *ex in-*

[75] Cf. *ASS,* VII, 572.

[76] *ASS,* VII, 572.

[77] C. 1854.

[78] C. 1889, § 1.

[79] C. 1573, § 2.

formata conscientia is invalid.[80] The reason urged by the Bishop in the case[81] in favor the suspension *ex informata conscientia* was the avoidance of scandal, arising from the fact that the cleric, during the appellation, continued to exercise his ministry. There are other means of avoiding the scandal besides taking an extraordinary remedy of suspension *ex informata conscientia,* which has been shown to be an improper remedy for such cases. If the suspension is a censure, then the appeal is *in devolutivo,*[82] and consequently there is no need of any other means to prevent scandal. But if it is concerned with a vindictive penalty, the appeal from which is *in suspensivo,*[83] other means are available. Although as a general rule, a sentence cannot be put into execution unless it is a *res judicata,*[84] still if there is an urgent grave necessity, a sentence, which is not yet *res judicata,* may be put into a provisory execution.[85] This legislation, it is true, is concerned primarily with contentious cases, as is evident from the wording of the law; however, it seems to be a guide to interpret similar canons dealing with criminal procedure. In canon 2222, § 2 an administrative removal from the exercise of the ministry, or a prohibition to exercise certain functions may be used by the Ordinary against a cleric in order to avoid scandal. The same means are offered to the Ordinary in the case of grave crimes; he may prohibit the cleric from the public reception of Holy Communion;[86] this means may be used any time during the course of the judicial process;[87] of course it must always be used with the limitations specified by law. It is not to the point here to examine these limitations, but it is sufficient to have pointed out the fallacy of the argument that in order to avoid scandal the Ordinary could proceed with the extraordinary remedy of suspension *ex informata conscientia.*[88] Since there are other measures which

[80] Cf. c. 1855, § 1.

[81] *ASS,* VII, 570.

[82] C. 2243, § 1.

[83] C. 1889, § 2.

[84] C. 1917, § 1.

[85] C. 1917, § 2.

[86] C. 1956.

[87] C. 1958.

[88] Although an appeal is pending, the Ordinary could suspend a cleric *ex informata conscientia* for an occult crime, which is different from the crime,

will sufficiently provide against any serious scandal, possibly arising in the matter, the conclusion follows that while an appeal is pending, the Ordinary cannot validly make use of the suspension *ex informata conscientia* to punish a crime, the condemnatory sentence of which is appealed.

4.

Canon 2192. Suspensio ex informata conscientia valet si ex pluribus delictis unum tantum fuerit occultum.

Although the cleric may have committed many crimes, and some of them are public, while perhaps only one is occult, nevertheless the cleric could be suspended *ex informata conscientia* on account of this one occult crime, since it is the purpose of the suspension *ex informata conscientia* to punish occult crimes.[89] This follows as a logical corollary to the legislation which says that a just and legitimate cause of the suspension *ex informata conscientia* is an occult crime. The cleric may be punished *ex informata conscientia* for an occult crime, while at the same time he may be punished by judicial process for his public crimes; the two penalties are distinct and may be imposed simultaneously or consecutively. A cleric may perhaps receive an absolutory sentence in a judicial trial, where he is accused of public crimes, but this absolutory sentence would have no bearing whatever on the suspension *ex informata conscientia* inflicted on account of an occult crime.[90]

concerning which the appeal is pending. Cf. Arndt, "Die Suspension,"—*AKKR*, 73 (1895), 153.

[89] Hinschius, *Kathol. Kirchenrechts*, V, 610; Pierantonelli, *Praxis Fori Ecclesiastici*, p. 288; *ASS*, VIII, 547; XIV, 372; XIX, 299.

[90] *"Quatenus censurae prolatae super pluribus delictis non sustineretur super unoquoque illorum, satis est quod ex uno tantum comprobarentur cum unumquodque sufficiens sit ad illas incurrendas."* Pignatelli, *Consultationes Canonicae*, IX, n. 5; cf. also Arndt, "Die Suspension Ex Informata Conscientia"—*AKKR*, 73 (1895), 154. After referring to this quotation from Pignatelli, Bassibey adds: *"C'est-à-dire lorsque l'évêque a basé son instruction sur le mélange de faits occultes et publics, les documents reposant sur des délits publics sont déclarés inutiles, renvoyés pour an action judiciaire, mais la sentence n'est pas invalidée, si les délits occultes allégués en même temps suffisent à la motiver."* "Des Sentences Ex Informata Conscientia,"—*JJC*, II (1893), 340.

CHAPTER VI

PROCEDURE

Canon 2187. Ad ferendam hanc suspensionem neque formae iudiciales neque canonicae monitiones requiruntur; sed satis est si Ordinarius, servato praescripto canonum qui sequuntur, simplici decreto declaret se suspensionem indicere.

In this canon a general norm of procedure is given. After stating what is not required, the Code simply states that the following canons constitute the law governing the procedure in the suspension *ex informata conscientia.* A judicial process or other judicial formalities are not required. Since the suspension *ex informata conscientia* is truly extrajudicial and extraordinary, the ordinary apparatus of a judicial process, or even the formalities of a summary trial are not necessary.[1] Therefore a previous accusation or *libellus petitionis* is not required; neither is the *citatio rei;* there is no *contestatio litis,* i.e., the declaration of the crime to the accused person with his contra-denial; witnesses need not necessarily be heard, and if heard are not necessarily examined according to the ordinary judicial requirements; however if witnesses are summoned, they are to be examined after the manner of taking testimony in a summary process. There is no opportunity necessarily given to the accused party to defend himself.[2] No sentence is given; in its place the Ordinary pronounces a decree, but this pronouncement is not done in a solemn judicial manner. However it would seem necessary that this decree be given in the presence of a notary. But by saying that these various formalities of a judicial process are not required, it is not meant that they are necessarily to be excluded;[3] it may be

[1] Cf. Molitor, *Kanonisches Gerichtsverfahren,* p. 226; Kober, *Die Suspension,* p. 73; Wernz-Vidal, *Jus Canonicum,* VI, n. 804.

[2] Such a proceeding is not contrary to justice. Cf. Bouix, *De Judiciis,* II, 339.

[3] However Smith warns: "The Bishop must take care not to make use of any formalities by which the crime will become public."—*Elements of Ecclesiastical Law,* II, n. 1311.

advisable to use some of them, but their use beyond the express requirements of the following canons, is within the discretion of the Ordinary.[4] Whether the Ordinary must use a regular process, if the cleric demands it, is not stated in the Code.[5] Since however the final discretion in the matter of judging the opportuneness of the use of this extraordinary measure is reserved to the Ordinary, provided of course the conditions required by law are present, and the right of recourse to the Holy See is kept in mind, it can be maintained that the Ordinary would not be under obligation to use a regular process, even though it were demanded by the cleric who is to be suspended.

Article I—Proofs

Canon 2190. Ordinarius, qui fert suspensionem ex informata conscientia, debet ex peractis investigationibus tales collegisse probationes, quae eum certum reddant clericum delictum revera perpetrasse et quidem adeo grave ut eiusmodi poena coercendus sit.

The Ordinary who inflicts a suspension *ex informata conscientia* must be certain because he is to act only from an informed conscience. He must be certain that a cleric really committed a crime, which is to be punished by so grave a penalty. The gravity of the crime must be weighed, and the penalty inflicted only in proportion to the gravity of the crime. In the last chapter the gravity of the crime was considered; in this article it will be necessary only to consider the proofs of the crime, and the manner of obtaining these proofs.

Although it is explicitly stated in canon 2187 that no judicial formalities are necessary, it is evident from the nature of the case, that the Ordinary is not exempted from the obligation of any process whatever; he cannot proceed arbitrarily in this important matter.[6]

[4] *"Will aber der Bischof einzeln Formen des ordentlichen oder summarischen Processes anwenden, so mag er es immerhin thun."*—Molitor, *Kanonisches Gerichtsverfahren*, p. 226. Cf. also Bouix, *De Judiciis*, II, 339; Heiner, *Katholisches Kirchenrecht*, p. 97; Wernz-Vidal, *Jus Canonicum*, VI, n. 804.

[5] Cf. Haring, *Katholischen Kirchenrechts*, II, 912.

[6] The Code warns the ordinary to proceed *"Sobrie et magna cum circumspectione"* in inflicting penalties. Cf. c. 2214, 2241, 2242.

The fundamental obligation of the Ordinary is that he be certain of his reasons before proceeding to the suspension. This fundamental obligation would be present even though there were no explicit law requiring it, because even by the natural law, the Ordinary is forbidden to punish a person unless he is certain that the punishment is merited. However canon 2190 explicitly sets forth this obligation, and requires that before proceeding to the suspension *ex informata conscientia,* the Ordinary collect such proofs as will render him certain.

Since the suspension *ex informata conscientia* is ordinarily concerned with an occult crime, the Ordinary in making the necessary investigations, should proceed secretly.[7] Even before the Code it was maintained that the investigation be made through an inquisition,[8] and this method still appears as the most satisfactory.[9] Although, as has been said, the investigation is to be secret, and the judicial forms are not prescribed, it will be advisable to make the inquisition according to the general norms of inquisition, in as far as possible.[10] Even as the whole proceeding, likewise the inquisition is extra-judicial and not a part of a criminal judicial procedure. This inquisition, since it is concerned with a crime which is not notorious and furthermore not certain, is a special inquisition.[11] The conduct of a specal inquisition in the case of a crime, of which the Ordinary is not certain, is a matter left to the prudent judgment of the Ordinary, who forms this judgment after word of some kind has reached him concerning the occult crime of a cleric.[12] Here it is well to bear in mind that no attention is to be paid to a denunciation made by a manifest enemy of the cleric, or by a wicked person or an untrustworthy one; nor to any anonymous denunciation, which in the circumstances, unless other elements are present, does not ren-

[7] Cf. Peries, *La Procédure Canonique,* p. 190; Bourret, *Des Sentences,* p. 92; Droste-Messmer, *Canonical Procedure,* p. 163.

[8] Cf. Bouix, *De Judiciis,* II, 350; Lega, *De Judiciis Ecclesiasticis,* IV, n. 400.

[9] Cf. Wernz-Vidal, *Jus Canonicum,* VI, n. 804; Suarez, *De Remotione Parochorum,* p. 241.

[10] Cf. c. 1939 and following canons.

[11] C. 1939.

[12] C. 1942, § 1.

der the accusation very probable.[13] In making this investigation, care should be taken to weigh the evidence, and only the testimony of reputable witnesses should be considered, and then only when the witnesses testify *ex propria scientia* and not from hearsay.[14] The Ordinary can make this inquisition himself or he can by special mandate commission someone else to make it. If he chooses to make this inquisition through another, he should choose a prudent and discreet person, preferably a priest.[15] The delegate must take an oath of secrecy.[16] However whether the Ordinary proceeds personally or through another all publicity should be avoided, and the utmost precaution used, lest the good name of the party, whether innocent or guilty, be injured.[17] For this reason it will be well to make witnesses promise under oath not to reveal either their disposition or even the fact of their examination.[18] In admitting witnesses, the Ordinary should require them to take an oath concerning the testimony which they give.[19] One oath, covering the different phases of the matter is sufficient, but it should be explicit enough to impress upon the witness its full obligation. Thus immediately upon calling them, the Ordinary can demand that the witness swear that they will tell the truth, and that they promise under oath that they will not reveal to anyone the fact that they have given testimony, or the nature of the matter of which they testified. After the Ordinary has gathered proofs, whether he or his delegate performed the investigation, he must duly study them and judge whether they are sufficient to warrant him to proceed with the suspension *ex informata conscientia*.[20]

[13] C. 1942, § 1.

[14] Cf. Vermeersch-Creusen, *Epitome*, III, n. 377; Roberti, *De Processibus*, II, 76.

[15] Cf. Vermeersch-Creusen, *Epitome*, III, n. 371.

[16] Cf. C. 1941, § 2.

[17] Cf. C. 1943; Boriero, *Manuale Processo Canonico*, p. 454; Bourret, *Des Sentences*, p. 92; Peries, *La Procédure Canonique*, p. 12; Droste-Messmer, *Canonical Procedure*, p. 162.

[18] Cf. Droste-Messmer, *Canonical Procedure*, p. 163.

[19] *Testes nisi iurati ne admittantur*.—C. 2145, § 2. Cf. Wernz-Vidal, *Jus Canonicum*, VI, n. 804.

[20] "*Episcopus magna prudentia in hac re se gerere debet, nec rumoribus in vulgus diffusis, aut delationibus aures facile praebere, minusque fidem adhi-*

In some cases there may be no necessity of a special inquisition, since sufficient arguments and proofs are deduced from the general investigation,[21] e.g., in the case where the suspension may be imposed for public crimes. Again in cases of public crimes it may happen the special investigation is instituted with the strict legal formalities, looking to the preparation for a judicial process, but from this the certainty of the crime becomes apparent, as also the presence of one of the circumstances which make a judicial process impossible; in which case the Ordinary may proceed to the suspension *ex informata conscientia.*[22]

After treating of the method of collecting the necessary proofs for the crime to be punished, Peries offers the following practical advice:

"The following suggestion will, we think, be useful to any individual bishop and enable him to keep all the proceedings secret, whilst it will, at the same time furnish him with a memorandum of all the evidence he may be asked to produce if the case is carried to Rome. After the examination of the accused and of the witnesses, the bishop himself should draw up a summary of all the facts, elicited in evidence, taking special care to note the dates and all points confirming the direct testimonies. . . . In addition to these depositions and documents bearing on the case, he will add his own observations and make out a brief statement of the leading points, if possible in a manner which will be intelligible to himself alone. He should enclose all this in a sealed envelope, noting on the outside the date of the suspension and its duration. Such memorandum should not be put among the official papers and documents of the diocese; but should be considered as belonging to the private papers of the bishop.[23] If no appeal be lodged against the sentence,[24] the bishop

bere occultis, ac secretis quarundam praesertim personarum accusationibus, quae odio, ira ac zeloptia agunt." Vecchioti, *Institutiones Canonicae,* II, 241.

[21] There are two kinds of inquisition, a general and a special. As the name implies, a general inquisition or investigation is one concerned with a wider and more extensive investigation, e.g., whether in this diocese certain crimes are being committed and by whom; while a special inquisition is a more limited and intensive investigation, e.g., whether this particular person committed this particular crime of which he is accused.

[22] Cf. Suarez, *De Remotione Parochorum,* p. 241.

[23] Peries and Droste-Messmer, who insist that these informations are not to be entered in the Archives, base their opinion on an express prohibition of the S. C. C., 11 aug. 1758—*Analecta Juris Pontificii,* XX, 68; since however

should destroy all such notes on the day on which the suspension expires.[25] If the bishop should die in the meantime, the suspension ceases by the very fact,[26] and all the papers bearing on the case should be destroyed by the administrator, who is positively forbidden to read them, or to make any use whatever of them." [27]

The Ordinary in gathering his proofs from this investigation, should get such proofs, which not only will make him certain of the crime and its gravity, but which will also be able to convince the Holy See of the crime, if the suspended cleric should have recourse to the Holy See.[28]

COROLLARY. PRIVATE KNOWLEDGE

Concerning the necessity of sufficient proofs, which the Ordinary must have of the guilt of the cleric, the question arises as to the sufficiency of the private knowledge of the Ordinary. Is it necessary that the proofs which are sufficient to convince the Ordinary of the

the Code is silent on the question, the general norm of the Code must be followed, which requires that all secret documents dealing with criminal matters be entered in the Secret Archives of the Diocese. Cf. c. 379, § 1; also Wernz-Vidal, *Jus Canonicum,* VI, n. 804.

[24] The author here is not using strictly canonical language; the suspension *ex informata conscientia* is not given *per sententiam,* and no appeal is possible; recourse is meant.

[25] If the suspension is a censure, these notes should be destroyed as soon as absolution is given.

[26] The author probably has in mind only vindictive penalties given *ad beneplacitum nostrum.* Censures do not cease by the death of the person inflicting them.

[27] "Suspension Ex Informata Conscientia,"—*ER,* XV (1896), 203.

[28] *"Eae probationes sunt afferendae quae per se aptae sunt ut penes alios viros honestos et peritos . . . plenam fidem faciant de crimine commisso."*—Wernz-Vidal, *Jus Canonicum,* VI, n. 804. The Sacred Congregation gives an apt warning on this subject: *"Meminerint vero Praesules, quod si contra decretum quo irrogata fuit suspensio promoveatur recursus ad Apostolicam Sedem tunc apud ipsam comprobari debet culpa quae eidem dedit occasionem. Consulto idcirco erit ut antequam haec poena infligatur, probationes illius, quantumvis extrajudicialiter et secreto colligantur; ita ut eo ipso quod cum omni certitudine culpabilitatis in punitione inferenda proceditur, si deinde causa examinanda est apud Apostolicam Sedem, probationes criminis in eas difficultates haud impingant quae ut plurimum occurrunt, in istiusmodi iudiciis."* Instr. S. C. de P. F., *Collectanea,* n. 1628.

crime and its gravity, be acquired from others, e.g., by investigation of witnesses, or can the Ordinary proceed with a suspension *ex informata conscientia* if he alone knows of the crime? This was a much-mooted question before the Code, and in general it can be said that the authors commonly maintained that the Ordinary should not proceed with a suspension *ex informata conscientia* unless he could prove to the satisfaction of the Holy See, by witnesses or documents, that the cleric was really guilty of the crime in question.[29] Bouix and others taught that the Ordinary could not proceed if he had only private knowledge, but for the validity of the suspension such proofs were necessary as would convince the Holy See.[30] Bouix based his position upon an analogy to the judicial process, where at least two witnesses are required, and where the judge cannot condemn a person from private knowledge. His second argument rested on the right of the cleric to have recourse to the Holy See; since recourse to the Holy See is allowed, it is the right of the Holy See to judge whether the arguments were sufficient or not, and the Holy See would judge whether the arguments convince itself, and not whether the arguments might have convinced the Ordinary.[31] D'Annibale on the other hand maintained the validity of a suspension based only on the private knowledge of the Ordinary, and this because of the very nature of the suspension, as being inflicted from an informed conscience;[32] he pointed out that the conscience of the Ordinary could be informed in various ways, whether from the revelation of others, or from his own observations.[33]

However in the past it is certain that the Holy See did not uphold suspensions *ex informata conscientia* when the proofs were not sufficient to convince it of the certainty of the crime in question, and

[29] Cf. Arndt, "Die Suspension ex Informata Conscientia,"—*AKKR,* 73 (1893), 157; Droste-Messmer, *Canonical Procedure,* p. 160.

[30] Cf. Bouix, *De Judiciis,* II, 346; Bourret, *Des Sentences,* p. 93; Peries. *La Procédure Canonique,* p. 193; Boriero, *Manuale Processo Canonico,* p. 454; et alii.

[31] These arguments are developed at great length, and are proposed in a very convincing manner by Bouix, *De Judiciis,* II, 346-350.

[32] This argument is perhaps developed best by Bassibey, "Des Sentences Ex Informata Conscientia,"—*JJC,* II (1893), 159-160.

[33] Cf. D'Annibale, *Summula Theologiae Moralis,* I, 385.

for this reason authors taught that practically the Ordinary should abstain from inflicting this suspension unless he had such proofs as would convince the Holy See.[34]

It has been shown that considerable uncertainty existed on this question previous to the Code. Not all authors would admit that suspensions based on the private knowledge alone were invalid. Consistently, however, they advised against their use in such cases. Does the Code settle the question? The Code uses the same terminology as was common before, calling this suspension a decree *ex informata conscientia.* It explicitly commands that before inflicting a suspension *ex informata conscientia,* the Ordinary should collect such proofs from investigations, which will render him certain of the crime,[35] and that if the cleric has recourse to the Holy See, the Ordinary must forward to the Holy See such proofs as will show that the cleric actually committed a crime which can be punished by this extraordinary penalty.[36] In spite of this seemingly clear legislation of the Code, some authors maintain even now that the question is unsettled,[37] and consequently it is necessary to examine in detail the arguments in support of either opinion. A study of the question warrants the conclusion that suspensions *ex informata conscientia* inflicted upon the basis of private knowledge only are both illicit and invalid.[38]

There are two ways in which an Ordinary may become certain of the commission of a crime, either by the testimony of others, or by his own observation whether this be by actual sight of the crime, or by a private confession made to him by the guilty person.[39] If the certainty of the Ordinary is based on the testimony of others, it is clear that the proofs must be such as to convince the Holy See. Although in canon 2190 the law simply requires that such proofs be gathered as will convince the Ordinary of the guilt, the nature of

[34] Cf. De Angelis, *Praelectiones Juris Canonici,* IV, 58; also the Instr. S. C. de P. F.—*Collectanea,* n. 1628.

[35] C. 2190.

[36] C. 2194.

[37] Vermeersch-Creusen, *Epitome,* III, n. 377; Suarez, *De Remotione Parochorum,* p. 244.

[38] Cf. Ferreres, *Institutiones Canonicae,* II, n. 941.

[39] Cf. Bouix, *De Judiciis,* II, 346.

the case presupposes that the proofs will also be able to convince other prudent men.[40] For in case of recourse, the Ordinary must forward the proofs to the Holy See, where they will be considered objectively. In examining the proofs, the Holy See is not interested in the subjective attitude of the Ordinary, but in the objective value of the arguments offered, and consequently inquires not whether the Ordinary was subjectively convinced of the crime, but whether the arguments given are sufficient to actually prove with certainty that the crime was committed. If the arguments do not objectively prove the case against the cleric, no matter what may be the personal opinion of the Ordinary, the suspension will not be upheld.[41] Consequently if the knowledge of the Ordinary is based on the testimony of others, he can proceed with a suspension *ex informata conscientia* validly and licitly, only when he has collected such proofs as will prove the crime to the satisfaction of the Holy See.

The second manner in which the Ordinary may acquire certainty of a crime is by personal observation, either as an eye witness or by secret confession.[42] The case, in which the Ordinary will be the only eye witness to the commission of a crime meriting the suspension *ex informata conscientia,* while still within the range of possibility, is without sufficient probability to render it practical.[43] The matter of secret confession however is more probable. Here it must be emphasized that there is no question whatever of sacramental confession; that a sacramental confessional knowledge can not be used by the Ordinary against a penitent is manifest from the very nature of the obligation, and needs no additional proof. It is well to remember also that there is no question of a judicial confession, since a formal judicial confession renders the crime notorious, and thus takes it beyond the scope of the suspension *ex informata conscientia.* The case therefore is limited to an extrasacramental, ex-

[40] Cf. Wernz-Vidal, *Jus Canonicum,* VI, n. 804.

[41] Cf. Peries, "Suspension Ex Informata Conscientia,"—*ER,* XV (1896), 201; Droste-Messmer, *Canonical Procedure,* p. 160; Bourret, *Des Sentences,* p. 94.

[42] "*Fieri potest ut Episcopus certus sit de hoc Titii delicto, ex eo quod ipse oculis propriis testis fuerit; item ex eo quod extrajudicialiter et in privato colloquio delictum illud Titius ipsi confessus fuerit.*"—Bouix, *De Judiciis,* II, 346.

[43] Cf. Suarez, *De Remotione Parochorum,* p. 243.

trajudicial confession made by the guilty cleric to the Ordinary.[44] Various circumstances might induce such a cleric to make this secret confession to the Ordinary, either *motu proprio* or upon the interrogation of the Ordinary. Since there is no doubt as to the commission of the crime, and its imputability, it would seem at first sight proper to maintain that in such a case the Ordinary could proceed with a suspension *ex informata conscientia.* Basing an argument on the seeming justification of the suspension, authors point out the propriety of punishing the cleric: it is certain he has committed a grave wrong; it is impossible to punish him in any other way, and since it is not to the best interest of the sanctity of the Church and the dignity of the clergy, that he remain unpunished, the Ordinary may punish him by a suspension *ex informata conscientia.*[45] The argument sounds plausible, but: the suspension *ex informata conscientia* is an extraordinary power given to the Ordinary, and rather an exception to the ordinary norms of criminal procedure; as an extraordinary and exceptional measure, it must be interpreted strictly and may not be interpreted to comprehend greater possibilities than the grant of it warrants;[46] but nowhere in the Code is the Ordinary granted power to proceed with a suspension on private knowledge only; *"nam secus posset quilibet iniquus judex extrajudicialiter procedendo, quoslibet innocentes opprimere; cum semper ipsi praesto esse praetextus se de patrato delicto privatam scientiam et convictionem habere."*[47] On the other hand, it is clearly the mind of the legislator to exclude this case. In canon 2190 it is explicitly stated that before proceeding to this extreme measure the Ordinary should acquire certain proofs of the 'crime' *ex peractis investigationibus*—clearly implying that private knowledge is not sufficient but that the Ordinary is to acquire his knowledge from investigations.[48]

[44] Cf. Wernz-Vidal, *Jus Canonicum,* VI, n. 454, 455; Roberti, *De Processibus,* II, 38.

[45] Icard, *Praelectiones S. Sulpitii,* III, 109; Peries, *La Procédure Canonique,* p. 193.

[46] "Every departure from common law is to be interpreted in its rigorous sense, especially if it be a case, as is the one we consider, called in canonical language *a jure exorbitans.*"—Peries, "Suspension Ex Informata Conscientia,"—*ER,* XV, (1896), 199.

[47] Bouix, *De Judiciis,* II, 348.

[48] Cf. Augustine, *A Commentary,* VII, 471.

Furthermore the suspended cleric has the right of recourse to the Holy See. In canon 2194 the Ordinary is required to forward such proofs as he has to the Holy See; but certainly the word of the Ordinary, as sole witness, is not a sufficient argument of proof.[49] The cleric denies the crime, and denies the confession of it; there is consequently merely the statement of the Ordinary and its denial by the cleric. The sufficiency of one witness to a crime is never recognized by ecclesiastical law, unless there is grave circumstantial evidence to the same fact;[50] but in the case under consideration there is no circumstantial evidence, because the supposition is that the only proof of the Ordinary is the secret confession made to him by the cleric.[51] It is therefore logical to conclude that the Holy See would immediately annul such a suspension,[52] as being unfounded, since no conclusive evidence of the crime has been presented.[53] The mind of the legislator, requiring the proofs of the Ordinary, is that the suspension can be inflicted only when the Ordinary is certain of the crime, with the certainty based upon proofs which will render the Holy See certain in the case of recourse.[54] Consequently the Ordinary cannot licitly or validly suspend *ex informata conscientia* from private knowledge only.[55] The

49 " . . . *et hoc etiamsi ipse Ordinarius iurans clerici delictum affirmet.*" —Bevilacqua, *De Episcopi seu Ordinarii Juribus ac Obligationibus*, n. 1581.

50 Cf. C. 1791, § 2.

51 An extrajudicial confession is not full proof. Cf. Wernz-Vidal, *Jus Canonicum*, VI, n. 455; Roberti, *De Processibus*, II, 38.

52 Cf. Ferreres, *Institutiones Canonicae*, II, n. 941; Augustine, *A Commentary*, VII, 471; Bevilacqua, *De Episcopi seu Ordinarii Juribus ac Obligationibus*, n. 1581.

53 The argument advanced by Icard, *Praelectiones S. Sulpitii*, III, 109, that the reputation of the Ordinary, in view of his prudence and integrity, would be considered as sufficient proof by the Sacred Congregation, is not conclusive. This would be tantamount to refusing a person suspended *ex informata conscientia* the right of recourse. Cf. Peries, "Suspension ex Informata Conscientia," —*ER*, XV (1896), 202.

54 ". . . *oportet ut numero et qualitate testium ordinarium sententian suam defendere possit.*"—Vermeersch-Creusen, *Epitome*, III, n. 377; ". . . *requiruntur probationes quas Ordinarius coram Sancta Sedes affere possit.*"—Bouuaert-Simenon, *Manuale*, n. 1235.

55 Ferreres, *Institutiones Canonicae*, II, n. 941; Bouuaert-Simenon, *Man-*

statement—canons 2190 and 2194 requiring the proofs do not exclude the case of private knowledge since these canons are concerned only with *communiter contingentibus*[56]—is in view of the strict interpretation required by the nature of the suspension *ex informata conscientia* not convincing. In attempting to give a too extensive interpretation of this power of the Ordinary, there is danger of giving to the Ordinary an arbitrary power,[57] which could easily lead to excessive abuses. It certainly is better that a few guilty clerics go unpunished than that justice should be endangered and jeopardized by putting into the hands of the Ordinary an almost unlimited power.[58]

"Reprehensibilis esset episcopus, si in sua synodo declararet, se deinceps ex privata tantum scientia poena suspensionis a divinis animadversurum in clericos, quos graviter deliquisse compererit, quamvis eorum delictum non possit in foro externo concludenter probari aut illud non expediat in aliorum notitiam deduci. Ejusmodi si quidem constitutio quandam deoleret ambitionem atque potestatis ostentationem ipseque episcopus traduceretur veluti in superbiam elatus, quasi vellet tantum in clerum sibi dominatum adstruere, qui in exosam degenerat tyrannidem." [59]

In view of this, and all the arguments offered above, the conclusion is warranted that a suspension *ex informata conscientia* inflicted from the private knowledge, unsubstantiated by evidential proofs, is both illicit and invalid. This conclusion is upheld as being in keeping with the spirit of the Church, which is ever thoughtful of protecting the rights of the least of her children.

uale, n. 1237; Cocchi, *Commentarium*, IV, 645; Bevilacqua, *De Episcopi seu Ordinarii Juribus ac Obligationibus*, n. 1581.

[56] Suarez, *De Remotione Parochorum*, 245; Vermeersch-Creusen, *Epitome*, III, n. 377; Bouuaert-Simenon, *Manuale*, n. 1235.

[57] ". . . it is equivalent to placing an innocent person in the impossibility of clearing himself, and condemning him to bear an unjust and unmerited punishment without hope or power of appeal."—Peries, "Suspension Ex Informata Conscientia,"—*ER*, XV (1896), 202.

[58] Cf. Bevilacqua, *De Episcopi seu Ordinarii Juribus ac Obligationibus*, n. 1581.

[59] Cf. Benedict XIV, *De Synodo Dioecesana*, Lib. XII, c. 8, n. 6; also Instr. S. C. de P. F.—*Collectanea*, n. 1628; Arndt, "Die Suspension Ex Informata Conscientia,"—*AKKR*, 73 (1893), 155.

Article II—The Canonical Admonitions

Neque requiruntur canonicae monitiones.[60] The canonical admonitions are never required.[61] That they are not required when there is question of the suspension *ex informata conscientia* as a vindictive penalty follows from the evident meaning of the words of canon 2187, which certainly must be applied to vindictive penalties; from the very nature of the vindictive penalty it is evident that there is no need of the canonical admonitions; a vindictive penalty has for its primary purpose the expiation of a crime already committed, while the purpose of the admonition is either to prevent the commission of a crime, or to induce the repentance of the delinquent; the vindictive penalty is not concerned directly with disposition of the delinquent, whether penitent or persevering in his evil intent.

A question may be raised however as to the necessity of the canonical admonitions when the suspension *ex informata conscientia* is a censure; in general, censures may not be inflicted unless preceded by the canonical admonitions. Does the suspension *ex informata conscientia* constitute an exception to this general rule? The answer seems to be in the affirmative.[62] The words of canon 2187—*neque canonicae monitiones requiruntur*—are general and no distinction is made between the suspension *ex informata conscientia* as a vindictive penalty and as a censure. In the following canon, where a distinction is made, the manifestation of the cause is required in the case of the suspension *ex informata conscientia* as a censure, while nothing is said concerning the canonical admonitions. It must be held therefore that if this suspension is a censure, the canonical admonitions are not required, unless it can be shown from the nature of the censure that the canonical admonitions are always necessary and can in no case be absent.

The general rule of censures is that for inflicting censures *ferendae*

[60] C. 2187. Cf. S. C. C., *Perusina,* 26 sept. 1795—*Thesaurus Resolutionum,* LXIV, 196 S. C. C., *Lucionen.,* 8 apr. 1848—*ASS,* XIV, 299.

[61] They may however be used. "*Neque canonica monitio excluditur, si hac forte via reus ad delictum non protrahendum vel reparandum adduci potest.*"—Vermeersch-Creusen, *Epitome,* III, n. 374.

[62] Cf. Blat, *Commentarium,* IV, n. 794.

sententiae the admonitions are required;[63] the reason of this general rule is found in the Code. Since the purpose of censures is to break the contumacy of the delinquent,[64] it is necessary to be certain that the delinquent is really contumacious; if a person, after being admonished, recedes from his contumacy, or if he is willing to do penance for his crime and to repair the damages or scandal resultant from his actions, he is no longer contumacious and consequently the censure cannot be inflicted upon him.[65] Under the old law, a triple admonition or warning was required, so that at least six days were consumed by these warnings, although under special circumstances, an exception was made and peremptory admonitions were allowed.[66] Now however under the Code law this triple admonition is no longer required; nor is any definite time necessary before the infliction of the censure; it is left to the prudent judgment of the Ordinary to decide how much time, if any, is to be allowed to the delinquent in which to recede from his contumacy.[67] In censures *latae sententiae* the canonical ȧdmonitions are not required, but the morally imputable violation of a sanctioned law is sufficient to incur these censures.[68] In these cases the sanction which is attached to the law is considered sufficient warning, and thus the knowledge of the law and the sanctions serves as the canonical *monitio,* without the necessity of a canonical admonition in the strict sense of the word.

From this it can be deduced that canonical admonitions are not necessarily always required before a censure can be incurred, and that consequently a law which would permit the infliction of a censure without canonical warnings is not impossible; it must be maintained that such a law is possible, without destroying the legal notion of a censure, and therefore if such a law is made, it is to be interpreted in its proper and literal sense. Since therefore canon 2187 states simply that canonical admonitions are not required in the suspension *ex informata conscientia,* and the canon does not distinguish between the suspension as a vindictive penalty and as a

[63] C. 2233, § 3.
[64] C. 2242, § 1.
[65] C. 2242, § 2, § 3.
[66] Cf. Santi-Leitner, *Praelectiones Juris Canonici,* I, n. 51.
[67] C. 2233. § 2.
[68] C. 2242, § 2.

censure,[69] there is no reason to recede from its obvious meaning, but rather to accept it in its natural sense, and maintain that also in the case of the suspension *ex informata conscientia* as a censure the canonical admonitions are not required.[70] The manifestation of the cause of the suspension however is strictly required, and further the Ordinary is urged to use paternal admonitions, as will be shown in the following article.

Article III—Manifestation of the Cause

Canon 2193. Prudenti Ordinarii arbitrio relinquitur suspensionis causam seu delictum clerico patefacere aut reticere, pastorali tamen adhibita solicitudine et caritate, ut, si delictum clerico manifestare censuerit, poena, ex paternis quae interposuerit monitis, nedum ad expiationem culpae, verum etiam ad emendationem delinquentis et ad occasionem peccati eliminandam inserviat.

As early as 1643 the Sacred Congregation decided that the Ordinary was not obliged to reveal the cause of the suspension to the suspended person.[71] The same idea was definitely established in the oft-quoted instructions of the Congregation in 1884, where it was explicitly stated that it was left to the prudent judgment of the Prelate to reveal or conceal the cause of the suspension to the delinquent; but if he revealed the cause, he was also to use paternal admonitions to promote the correction of the delinquent and to remove the occasion of sin. Some canonists still held that if the suspension *ex informata conscientia* was imposed as a censure the canonical

69 "*Mais la text est formel et absolu suspensi, ne distinguant pas entre les deux façons de procéder.*"—Bassibey, "Des Sentences,"—*JJC*, II (1893), 153.

70 However prudence as well as charity may demand the canonical admonitions. Cf. Droste-Messmer, *Canonical Procedure*, p. 163; Pierantonelli, *Praxis Fori Ecclesiastici*, tit. VII, n. 4.

71 Cf. S. C. C., *Vercellen.*, 21 mart. 1643—*Fontes*, n. 2642; S. C. C., *Capritana*, 16 dec. 1730—*Fontes*, n. 3368; S. C. C., *Oritana*, 20 aug. 1735—Pelella, *Declarationes et Resolutiones*, p. 87; Benedict XIV, *De Synodo Dioecesana*, Lib. XII, c. 8, n. 4; Bourret, *Des Sentences*, p. 96; Bouix, *De Judiciis*, II, 332; Wernz-Vidal, *Jus Canonicum*, VI, n. 804.

admonitions were necessary.[72] The Code follows the Instruction of the Sacred Congregation.

In a previous canon it had already been decreed that the canonical admonitions are unnecessary, but that the cause of the crime had to be revealed if the suspension was imposed as a censure.[73] But if the suspension is imposed as a vindictive penalty, it is evident from the wording of canon 2193 that the Ordinary is not obliged to manifest the cause of the suspension *ex informata conscientia* to the delinquent.[74] It is left to his prudent judgment to manifest the cause or to be silent concerning it, and this is tautamount to saying that the suspension *ex informata conscientia* can always be inflicted as a vindictive penalty,[75] because canon 2188, 2° clearly requires for the validity of the suspension, the manifestation of the cause if the suspension is a censure. The clause introduced by *dummodo* is necessary for the validity.[76] Furthermore the very nature and purpose of a censure demand the manifestation of the cause of a censure.[77] A censure is a medicinal penalty inflicted upon a person, with the purpose of breaking his contumacy and as soon as he recedes from his contumacy he is to receive absolution. But it is impossible to speak of a person remaining in contumacy, if he is ignorant of the cause of his punishment. It might be argued that his conscience would inform him sufficiently when he was being punished; but this is not necessarily true. Suppose that he had committed several crimes, and the Ordinary inflicted a suspension on him, without manifesting the cause; it could easily happen that the judgment of

[72] Cf. Lega, *De Judiciis Ecclesiasticis,* IV, n. 399; Bassibey, "Des Sentences"—*JJC,* II (1893), 153.

[73] C. 2188, 2°.

[74] Cf. S. C. C., *Lucionen.,* 8 apr. 1848, *ASS,* XIV, 299, where the reasons for not revealing the cause are stated by the advocate in the case: *Quocirca episcopus, ut arcanum sibi concreditum haud prodere videretur et parochi famae quodammodo consuleret, novumque etiam scandalum declinaret, recte sibi faciendum esse duxit, si tot, tantaque, deprehensa ex peracta inquisitioue, flagitia ipsi parocho reticeret.*

[75] Cf. Cance, *Le Code de Droit Canonique,* III, 309; Wernz-Vidal, *Jus Canonicum,* VI, n. 804.

[76] C. 39.

[77] Cf. Ferrares, *Bibliotheca,* verbo *suspensio,* n. 14; VIII, 519; cf. also Bourret, *Des Sentences,* p. 98.

the cleric would be in opposition to the judgment of the Ordinary, and the cleric might think that he was being punished for one crime, while in reality the Ordinary intended to punish him for another. It is evident therefore that the Ordinary must manifest the cause of the suspension, if it is a censure.[78]

The cause of the suspension must be manifested to the delinquent before the infliction of the suspension, although no appreciable length of time need intervene between the manifestation of the cause and the infliction of the censure. If the cleric recedes from his contumacy as soon as the cause is made known to him, can the Ordinary then impose the suspension? In this case the suspension can be imposed as a vindictive penalty, but not as a censure; [79] therefore if then the Ordinary inflicts the suspension, it is presumed to be a vindictive penalty, and not a censure.[80] However if it is evident that even then the Ordinary intends to inflict it as a censure, the presumption is that in the judgment of the Ordinary, the contumacy has not ceased; [81] and since it is his right to decide when the contumacy ceases, the suspension *ex informata conscientia* is valid at least *in foro externo*. However as soon as it is evident to the Ordinary that the cleric has receded from his contumacy, absolution must be given.[82]

It has been pointed out that the manifestation of the crime for which the suspension *ex informata conscientia* is inflicted, is essential to the alidity of the suspension, if it is imposed as a censure.[83] If the suspension is imposed as a vindictive penalty, the Ordinary is not obliged to manifest the cause of the suspension, but even in this case he may do so, unless other circumstances advise against such a revelation, e. g., the implication of a third party.[84] In every case,

[78] Cf. Bareille, *Code du Droit Canonique*, p. 560; Wernz-Vidal, *Jus Canonicum*, VI, n. 804.

[79] C. 2248, § 2.

[80] Cf. Wernz-Vidal, *Jus Canonicum*, VI, n. 804.

[81] C. 2242, § 3; cf. Suarez, *De Remotione Parochorum*, p. 233.

[82] C. 2248, § 2. This obligation of absolution is *ex justitia*. Cf. Blat, *Commentarium*, IV, n. 795.

[83] C. 2188, 2°.

[84] Cf. Vermeersch-Creusen, *Epitome, III*, n. 380. Cf. also Bouuaert-Simenon, *Manuale*, n. 1236.

when he does manifest the cause, he is urged also to administer paternal admonitions to the clerics: *Pastorali tamen, etc.* of canon 2193. Here the Code explicitly appeals to the pastoral solicitude and charity of the Ordinary. The deep mercy and kindness, which is evident on all occasions in the Church's dealing with those who have had the misfortune to fall into sin, is intensified in the case of unfortunate clerics, and like a loving mother, the Church appeals to those who must administer justice to temper their justice with mercy and kindness.[85] It is to be noted here that the Ordinary is to administer paternal admonitions, while previously it has been decreed that there is no obligation to use the canonical admonition; in fact, sometimes in view of the circumstances of secrecy,[86] the canonical admonitions are not in place. The paternal admonitions are administered as from a father to a son, based on charity, and not as a superior to an inferior or as a judge to an accused, based on justice.[87] It should therefore be given privately without any witnesses being present and given in such a manner as will prove beneficial to the cleric.[88] Kindness frequently succeeds very well in inducing a cleric to desist from his evil ways, and to lead a life in accord with clerical virtue. This gives the accused cleric a chance to explain his actions, and frequently his explanation may be of such a nature as to show that some mistake has occurred, and that the Ordinary is not to judge him too severely, but that in reality he has very little guilt in the matter. But even though he is fully guilty, kindness will keep him from continuing in his sin, and he will more easily accept the punishment, when it is thus shown to be beneficial

[85] Cf. Conc. Trid., Sess. XIII, cap. 1, *de reform.;* Giraldi, *Expositio Juris Pontificii,* Pars II, sect. 43; Bassibey, "Des Sentences Ex Informata Conscientia" —*JJC,* II (1893), 151.

[86] "To no one else may the Bishop make any revelations whatsoever. The crime is occult and its punishment should be the same."—Peries, "Suspension Ex Informata Conscientia"—*ER,* XV (1896), 250; cf. also Bourret, *Des Sentences,* p. 97.

[87] Cf. Droste-Messmer, *Canonical Procedure,* p. 150; Smith, *Elements of Ecclesiastical Law,* II, n. 1312.

[88] Cf. Peries, "Suspension Ex Informata Conscientia"—*ER,* XV (1896), 250; Wernz-Vidal, *Jus Canonicum,* VI, n. 804.

to him.[89] This paternal admonition may be given personally or by means of a letter.[90] There is no necessity to make a note of it and preserve this note in the Secret Archives.[91] The purpose of these paternal admonitions is not only to expiate the crime, which is really the proper purpose of vindictive penalties, but also to promote, according to the universal wish of the Church in inflicting penalties, the amendment of the sinner, and to remove the occasion of sin, so that it may not again be a stumbling block thwarting the perseverance of the penitent.[92]

Article IV—Mode of Suspension

The suspension *ex informata conscientia* is classified in the Code under the title of penal sanctions: thus in the general heading of the third part of Book 4, *De modo Procedendi in nonnullis expediendis negotiis vel sanctionibus poenalibus applicandis.* It is also called in the context a *remedy;* however, although expressly called a remedy, it is not to be confused with the penal remedies which are treated in canon 2306. It is called an extraordinary remedy in the sense that it is beyond the ordinary remedies against crime.

The suspension *ex informata conscientia* is truly a penalty; by this proper name it is expressly mentioned several times,[93] and from the whole context of the law, and the nature of the case, it is evident that the suspension *ex informata conscientia* is an ecclesiastical

[89] Icard, *Praelectiones* S. *Sulpitii,* III, 109—Peries, "Suspension Ex Informata Conscientia"—*ER,* XV (1896), 250.

[90] Cf. Arndt, "Die Suspension Ex Informata Conscientia,"—*AKKR,* 73 (1895), 158.

[91] Cf. Hergenroether, *Katholischen Kirchenrechts,* p. 366. On the other hand, Suarez, *De Remotione Parochorum,* p. 231, following Noval, "De Ratione Corrigendi"—*Just Pont.,* III (1923), 148, insists that a note of this admonition be made and preserved in the Secret Archives, basing the argument on canon 2309, § 5. This canon is concerned with canonical admonitions, public and private, and need not be applied to paternal admonitions. The opposite extreme is maintained by Droste-Messmer: "It is strictly forbidden, both morally and legally to enter a paternal admonition on the records of the chancery."—*Canonical Procedure,* p. 150.

[92] Cf. Blat., *Commentarium,* IV, n. 800; Arndt, "Die Suspension Ex Informata Conscientia,"—*AKKR,* 73 (1895), 159.

[93] CC. 2188, 2,° 2190, 2193.

penalty. It can be imposed only for a crime, and in general follows the laws governing penalties. There are two classes of penalties in the Code, medicinal and vindictive. In canon 2188, 2° it is expressly stated that suspension *ex informata conscientia* may be imposed also as a censure or medicinal penalty,[94] the *also* implies of course that it may be imposed as a vindictive penalty. The suspension *ex informata conscientia* can therefore be either a vindictive penalty or a censure, and in the individual case, its nature can be judged from the manner of inflicting it or from other circumstances. If it is imposed for a definite period or if the cause is not mentioned, it will be seen to be a vindictive penalty; [95] if on the other hand it is inflicted until a person repents, it is evidently a censure. In case of doubt, the suspension is presumed to be a censure; [96] however this presumption cedes to contrary proof; but as long as the doubt of its nature remains, the suspension should be considered a censure.[97] This suspension, whether it be a censure or a vindictive penalty, follows the general norm of penalties laid down in the Fifth Book of the Code.[98]

Whether in an individual case it will be better to impose this suspension as a censure or as a vindictive penalty cannot be determined by *a priori* reasoning, but must be prudently judged from the circumstances of the case.[99] In general it can be said that the medicinal effects of the penalty are more desired than the vindictive

[94] Before the Code some authors maintained that the suspension *ex informata conscientia* could be only a vindictive penalty. Cf. Bassibey, "Des Sentences Ex Informata Conscientia,"—*JJC*, II (1893), 156; Laemmer, *Katholischen Kirchenrechts*, 742.

[95] Cf. Wernz-Vidal, *Jus Canonicum*, VI, n. 801; Vermeersch-Creusen, *Epitome*, III, n. 375; De Meester, *Compendium*, III_2, n. 1681.

[96] C. 2255, § 2.

[97] *"Ratio est quia censurae difficilius incurruntur et facilius absolvuntur."*—Sole, *De Delictis et Poenis*, 142.

[98] Cf. Hinschius, *Kathol. Kirschenrechts*, V, 610; Wernz-Vidal, *Jus Canonicum*, VI, n. 804.

[99] *"Si la suspense ex informata conscientia est en punition d'un crime passé, il est recu qu'elle ne dépasse pas six mois. S'il s'agit d'un crime répété d'une habitude coupable, la suspense revêt le caractère d'une censure médicinale et peut être infligée indéfiniment."*—Vering, *Droit Canom*, II, 446; D'Annibale, *Summula Theologiae Moralis*, II, n. 384.

effects, since the Church is concerned primarily with the sanctification of the sinner.[100] However the common good frequently necessitates the use of vindictive penalties. Consequently it will be left to the prudent judgment of the Ordinary to decide in a given case, whether it is better to inflict the suspension *ex informata conscientia* as a censure or as a vindictive penalty. If the Ordinary judges it proper not to reveal the cause of the suspension to the delinquent, the only course open to him is to impose it as a vindictive penalty, since he must state the cause if it is imposed as a censure.[101] The Code in giving him the right to impose this suspension *ex informata conscientia* without revealing the cause, gives him the option of always inflicting it as a vindictive penalty.

Article V—The Decree of Suspension

Canon 2188. Hujusmodi decretum detur in scriptis, nisi adiuncta aliud exigant, designato die, mense et anno; in eoque:

1°. Expresse dicatur suspensionem ferri ex informata conscientia seu ex causis ipsi Ordinario notis;

2°. Indicetur tempus durationis poenae; abstineat autem Ordinarius ab ipsa infligenda in perpetuum. Potest vero infligi etiam tanquam censura, dummodo hoc in casu clerico patefiat causa propter quam suspensio irrogatur.

3°. Clare indicentur actus qui prohibentur, si suspensio non in totum sed ex parte infligatur.

In this canon the special norms of procedure which are required in the suspension *ex informata conscientia* are given. The suspension is not inflicted through a sentence, but by a simple decree: *satis est si Ordinarius . . . simplici decreto declaret se suspensionem indicere.*[102] The decree by which this suspension is inflicted, should be in writing unless unusual circumstances exist, e.g., if it is feared that

[100] Cf. Vermeersch-Creusen, *Epitome*, III, n. 380.

[101] Cf. Bourret, *Des Sentences*, p. 98; Ferraris, *Bibliotheca*, verbo *suspensio*, VII, 519; D'Annibale, *Summula Theologiae Moralis*, II, n. 384; Wernz-Vidal, *Jus Canonicum*, VI, n. 804; Vermeersch-Creusen, *Epitome*, III, n. 375.

[102] C. 2187.

the cleric would abuse the written decree to the damage of the Ordinary, or if its documentary form could involve the Ordinary in a civil process.[103] The time is to be definitely determined, i.e., the date on which it is issued, and its duration if it is a vindictive penalty. In the canon it is definitely stated that the suspension may also be imposed as a censure, and if so imposed, the cause of the censure must be manifested to the delinquent. The final number of the canon logically demands that if the suspension is inflicted partially, it must be clearly evident which acts are forbidden.

1. In Writing

The suspension *ex informata conscientia* must be inflicted by a written decree. In the original wording of the Tridentine law, nothing was specified concerning the necessity of putting this suspension in writing; the words used *quoquo modo, etc.*, indicated that no limitations were placed on the Ordinary, requiring that this decree be written. Consequently in various decisions of the Sacred Congregation, the validity of oral suspensions was upheld. However the Instruction of 1884 required that the suspension be given in writing. Whether this written decree was necessary for the validity of the suspension or not, was not unanimously held.[104] However the sounder view maintained that an oral decree of suspension *ex informata conscientia* was also valid. The Code has taken over the legislation of the Instruction of 1884, requiring that the decree be in writing, but takes cognizance of the fact that circumstances may arise which favor an oral suspension. Consequently in virtue of the present legislation, it cannot be maintained that a written decree is necessary for the validity of the suspension, but that generally the Ordinary is to use writing, unless good reasons persuade him to an oral decree of suspension. Such reasons may in rare circumstances

[103] Cf. Vermeersch-Creusen, *Epitome*, III, n. 375; Bouuaert-Simenon, *Manuale*, n. 1234.

[104] Among those insisting on writing for the validity may be mentioned Heiner, *Katholisches Kirchenrecht*, II, 95; Boriero, *Manuale Processo Canonico*, p. 449; Peries, "Suspension Ex Informata Conscientia"—*ER*, XV (1896), 15. Denying this may be mentioned: Bassibey, "Des Sentences Ex Informata Conscientia,"—*JJC*, II (1893), 155, and especially Pierantonelli, *Praxis Fori Ecclesiastici*, p. 235.

exist, but under normal conditions, the decree of suspension is to be in writing. If it is given orally, it should be in the presence of two witnesses.[105]

2. Date

The date on which the suspension is inflicted must be clearly indicated. The necessity of the date appearing on the decree of suspension is evident. If the suspension is imposed as a vindictive penalty, and not *in perpetuum,* it will cease with the lapse of the time for which it was imposed. But the date is also important, even though it is imposed as a censure, because the law imposes certain juridicial effects upon one who remains in censure and contumacy beyond a definite time. Thus in either case, the usefulness, and in fact, the necessity of the date is clear. However it cannot be said that the date is necessary for validity. There is no indication of an expressly invalidating clause here, and where the law does not expressly demand a condition for validity, the condition is demanded only for the liceity of the act. The date should be complete, the day, the month and the year; however the hour is not required.

3. Nature of the Suspension

The Code requires that express mention be made of the nature of the suspension: *Expresse dicatur suspensionem ferri ex informata conscientia seu ex causis ipsi Ordinario notis.* Since according to the general norms of procedure, the canonical admonitions must precede the infliction of a canonical penalty, except in the case of special gravity or of a grave scandal,[106] a cleric has a right to disregard a suspension inflicted upon him without these warnings.[107] In order therefore that the cleric be bound to recognize and accept the decree of suspension, he must know that the decree itself is valid, and a decree of such a nature will be valid only if it is imposed as suspension *ex informata conscientia.*[108] Consequently the decree must

[105] C. 2225.

[106] C. 2222, § 1.

[107] Cf. Smith, *Elements of Ecclesiastical Law,* II, n. 1312; Bourret, *Des Sentences,* p. 100; Vermeersch-Creusen, *Epitome,* III, n. 375.

[108] Cf. Bouix, De Judiciis, II, 340; Bassibey, "Des Sentences Ex Informata conscientia,"—*JJC,* II (1893), 154.

specify that it is given *ex informata conscientia,* or words to the same effect, e.g., *from causes known to the Ordinary.* It is advisable however to avoid the latter analogous terms, and state definitely and expressly that it is a suspension *ex informata conscientia.* No special formula is required.

4. Duration

Furthermore in the decree of the suspension, the duration of the penalty is to be noted. This legislation evidently deals with the suspension inflicted as a vindictive penalty, since as a censure, the duration of the suspension is not determined by the Ordinary inflicting it, but is determined rather by the delinquent, who must be absolved when he recedes from his contumacy.[109] The fact that the legislator first posits the necessity of specifying the duration of the suspension, and only afterwards, specifies that it may be inflicted also as a censure, is indicative of the mind of the legislator that the suspension *ex informata conscientia* is primarily to be used as a vindictive penalty,[110] although its use as a censure is entirely legitimate.

5. Partial Suspension

The Code requires that when the suspension is not general but only partial, it must be clearly indicated just what acts are forbidden. Since the various partial suspensions are clearly stated in the Code,[111] this can easily be done by simply using the specific canonical terms, which are proper to partial suspensions.[112]

Article VI—Formula

Although no particular formula is required, it will be convenient to follow a definite form in order to insure that nothing necessary to the validity of the decree is omitted. Various formulas are offered

[109] C. 2248, § 2; cf. Suarez, *De Remotione Parochorum,* p. 234.

[110] "*. . . ce qui montre que cette peine est en principe vindicative.*"—Cance, *Le Code de Droit Canonique,* III, 309.

[111] C. 2279.

[112] Creusen remarks that too great confidence is not to be placed in the knowledge of the cleric, and therefore "*potius indicanda est saltem species actuum qui prohibentur.*"—Vermeersch-Creusen, Epitome, III, n. 375; e.g. suspension from hearing confessions, or a suspension from saying Mass, etc.

by the authors.[113] The one offered below is borrowed from Mothon.[114]

Nos, N. N., gratia Dei et auctoritate Apostolicae Sedis Ordinarius N . . .

Dilecto Nobis in Christo, N. N.

Post diligentem et accuratam inquisitionem a Nobis peractam, ex informata conscientia, ob graves causas Nobis cognitas (Scilicet. . . .)[115] *virtute praesentium, auctoritate officii Nostri ordinaria, te dominum N. N. suspendimus ab . . . per . . . teque eo tempore suspensum a praedictorum exercitio officiorum, declaramus. In Nomine Patris et Filii et Spiritus Sancti. Amen.*

Datum . . . (city) sub signo sigilloque Nostro et subscriptione Nostri cancellarii die . . . mensis . . . anni . . .

............................*Episcopus N.*

Locus Sigilli.

De Mandato Ill^{mi} ac R^{mi} D. Ordinarii,

............................*Cancellarius.*

If the chancellor is not at the same time a notary, the decree should be signed in the presence of a notary,[116] who witnesses the signature of the Ordinary and likewise signs it. Two copies should be made, one copy to be preserved in the Secret Archives of the Diocese [117] and the other copy to be given to the cleric thus suspended. The Ordinary may deliver this decree of suspension to the cleric personally, or he may send it through the mail.[118] If it is sent

[113] Cf. Monacelli, *Formularium Legum*, Pars III, tit. II, form. 6; Muniz, *Procedimientos Eclesiasticos*, 1, n. 719.

[114] *Institutions Canoniques*, III, 111.

[115] The Ordinary has no obligation to manifest the cause, unless the suspension is a censure. Formerly authors taught that the Ordinary was not permitted to mention the cause in the decree itself; Cf. Smith, *Elements of Ecclesiastical Law*, II, n. 1312; Peries, "Suspension Ex Informata Conscientia," —*ER*, XV (1896), 251. However modern canonists permit the mention of the cause in the decree itself. Cf. Wernz-Vidal, *Jus Canonicum*, VI, n. 804.

[116] C. 2142; Cf. Ferreres, *Institutiones Canonicae*, II, n. 942.

[117] C. 2142.

[118] Although Droste-Messmer denied that this decree could be sent through the mail, the majority of canonists admit this procedure and rightly so.

through the mail, prudence will dictate that it be sent by means of a registered letter, with a return receipt demanded;[119] otherwise a cleric could deny that he received it. The letter should be delivered by the mailman to the cleric personally, and not to anybody else. In all cases where possible it would be well to have the copy of the decree which is deposited in the Secret Archives signed by the suspended cleric.[120]

The notary, who witnesses the document and who signs it, and likewise the witnesses in whose presence the decree is given orally,[121] are bound to secrecy, and are required to take an oath of secrecy.[122] While the Ordinary, giving the decree, does not have to take an oath of secrecy, he too has an obligation of secrecy.[123]

[119] Cf. cc. 1717, § 3 and 1877.

[120] Cf. Bourret, *Des Sentences,* p. 101.

[121] C. 2225.

[122] C. 2144, § 1.

[123] Cf. Bourret, *Des Sentences,* p. 101; Gennari, *Sulla Privazione del Beneficio Ecclesiastico,* p. 140.

CHAPTER VII

EFFECTS OF THE SUSPENSION

Article I—Duration

It has been noted in the previous chapter that in inflicting a suspension *ex informata conscientia* the Ordinary is obliged to specify the duration of the suspension in the decree itself. In order to have a comprehensive appreciation of the time element, which is an important phase of this extraordinary suspension, it will be necessary to consider three questions: Can this suspension be inflicted *in perpetuum?* If inflicted *ad beneplacitum nostrum,* how is it to be interpreted? What norm is offered by canonists?

1. Perpetual Suspensions

Abstineat autem Ordinarius ab ipsa infligenda in perpetuum [1]

The Ordinary is required to specify the duration of the suspension, if it is inflicted as a vindictive penalty. The suspenson is of the nature of a serious punishment, and since punishment in order to be just, must be proportionate to the crime, it is to be imposed only for a crime of a serious nature, and for a length of time proportionate to the offense. The Code, following the Instruction of 1884, explicitly forbids the Ordinary to inflict this suspension *in perpetuum.* It is clearly the mind of the legislator that this extraordinary measure is to be of a temporary nature, and not to be a perpetual punishment. If an Ordinary inflicts a suspension *ex informata conscientia* perpetually, he certainly acts illicitly but does he act invalidly? The question here is concerned with the suspension *ex informata conscientia* itself, whether if issued *in perpetuum* it is *ipso facto* invalid, and not with the question as to what the Holy See would do if recourse would be taken to it against such a decree. Whether in an individual case, the Holy See would declare such a decree null, or whether it would simply reduce the duration, is not the question here. Does the Code in prohibiting the suspension *ex informata*

[1] C. 2188, 2°.

conscientia from being inflicted *in perpetuum*, intend to invalidate such a suspension?

In view of the general norm of the Code that no law is to be considered invalidating unless the act is expressly or equivalently declared to be null,[2] there is no ground to consider the law in question invalidating, because the terms used do not expressly or equivalently declare the act null and void.[3] The word *abstineat* cannot be interpreted to mean *non potest;* such an interpretation would necessitate an unwarranted use of the word *abstineat*, used here in the subjunctive, implying a command to abstain, with no indication whatever of a more extensive meaning.[4]

The argument, sometimes advanced by authors,[5] in favor of the invalidity of such perpetual suspensions, is not conclusive.[6] They argue that a perpetual suspension is equivalent to privation of office or deposition.[7] It is clear from the Code that a perpetual suspension, which may sometimes be inflicted, is not the same as a privation of office or deposition, since all of these penalties are separately and distinctly admitted by the Code.[8] The most that can be adduced from such a comparison is an argument against the advisability of inflicting such perpetual suspensions, but not their invalidity.

An argument cannot be adduced from an interpretation of the

[2] C. 11.

[3] Cf. Augustine, *Commentary,* VII, 477.

[4] Bassibey, commenting on these words of the Instruction of 1884, aptly remarks: *"Il y a là une exhortatione excellente, une ligne de conduite fort sage que les évêques feront bien de suivre, mais il n'y a pas une loi formelle contre la loi de Trent."*—"Des Sentences Ex Informata Conscientia"—*JJC,* II (1893), 287.

[5] Arndt, "Die Suspension Ex Informata Conscientia,"—*AKKR,* 73 (1895), 164; Pierantonelli, *Praxis Fori Ecclesiastici,* 257; Bourret, *Des Sentences,* p. 105; Smith, *Elements of Ecclesiastical Law,* II, 1296; Wernz, *Jus Decretalium,* V, n. 898.

[6] Cf. Bassibey, "Des Sentences Ex Informata Conscientia,"—*JJC,* II (1893), 321.

[7] This argument and others are strongly urged by Vering, *Droit Canon,* II, 446; he maintains the invalidity of perpetual suspensions *ex informata conscientia,* and says that the contrary opinion is absurd and contrary to justice. Cf. also Pierantonelli, *Praxis Fori Ecclesiastici,* p. 257; Bourret, *Des Sentences,* p. 105.

[8] C. 2298. Cf. Suarez, *De Remotione Parochorum,* p. 236.

old law. There are explicit decisions of the Sacred Congregation upholding such a perpetual suspension *ex informata conscientia;*[9] while on the other hand there is no decision explicitly declaring that perpetual suspensions are invalid.[10] The prohibition contained in the Instruction of 1884 does not explicitly invalidate such suspensions.[11] The conclusion therefore is warranted that this law deals only with the liceity, and does not invalidate perpetual suspensions *ex informata conscientia.*[12] However this does not justify such suspensions, and it is clear that the Church does not favor them.[13] Further in the past the Sacred Congregation has reduced the duration of longer suspensions *ex informata conscientia,*[14] and the cleric against whom an Ordinary has issued such a perpetual suspension will obtain a cancellation or at least a reduction of the suspension by recourse to the Holy See.

2. *Ad Beneplacitum Nostrum*

The suspension *ex informata conscientia* may be inflicted *ad beneplacitum nostrum.* A question arises immediately, as to determining whether such a suspension is a censure or a vindictive penalty. Although some admit that such an expression lends itself to either interpretation,[15] it seems more reasonable to restrict it to the mean-

[9] S. C. C., *Nullius,* 3 feb. 1593: "*C. 1, Sess. XIV, de reform, locum habere in prohibitionibus et suspensionibus tam temporaneis quam perpetuis.*"—*Fontes,* n. 2254.

[10] The decisions ordinarily quoted in favor of invalidity are: S. C. C., *S. Severini,* 19 sept. 1778. *ASS,* XIV, 412; *Thesaurus Resolutionum,* XLVII, 47; S. C. C., *Placentina,* 26 feb. 1848—*Thesaurus Resolutionum,* CVIII, 49; S. C. C., *S. Agathae Goth.,* 26 feb. 1853—*Thesaurus Resolutionum,* CXII, 46. However none of these decisions give an absolute argument. Cf. Bouix, *De Judiciis,* II, 336, 337.

[11] The Instruction uses practically the same words as the Code.

[12] Cf. Vermeersch-Creusen, *Epitome,* III, n. 375; Cocchi, *Commentarium,* IV, 642.

[13] Cf. Droste-Messmer, *Canonical Procedure,* p. 161; *Analecta Juris Pontificii,* XIV, 1975; XIX, 1129; Giraldi, *Expositio Juris Pontificii,* Pars. II, Sect. 43; Lucidi, *De Visitatione SS.LL.,* I, 385; Smith, *Elements of Ecclesiastical Law,* II, n. 1316; Falco, *Codex Juris Canonici,* p. 271.

[14] Cf. Arndt, "Die Suspension Ex Informata Conscientia"—*AKKR,* 73 (1895), 168; Vermeersch-Creusen, *Epitome,* III, n. 375.

[15] Cf. Suarez, *De Remotione Parochorum,* p. 234.

ing of a vindictive penalty.[16] The ordinary meaning attached by canonists to the expression *ad beneplacitum nostrum* is that it means an indefinite time, to be terminated at the express will of the one so using it, or else that it terminates automatically with the loss of the power of the person using it.[17] Thus, if a suspension *ex informata conscientia* would be issued *ad beneplacitum nostrum,* it would cease at the death or loss of office of the Ordinary issuing it. That the suspension *ex informata conscientia* issued with such phraseology, is to be so interpreted is manifest from a decision of the Sacred Congregation.[18] Further the attempt to interpret such a suspension as a censure seems abortive, since censures are terminated only by absolution. Since this absolution is not left to the arbitrary discretion of the Ordinary, it must be given when one recedes from his contumacy; the termination of a censure therefore cannot strictly be said to be dependent in its duration upon the will of the Ordinary inflicting it *ad beneplacitum.*[19] The conclusion is warranted therefore that if a suspension *ex informata conscientia* is inflicted *ad beneplacitum nostrum,* it is a vindictive penalty, of a temporary nature, terminating *ipso facto* with the jurisdiction of the person who thus inflicts it. Since it is a vindictive penalty, it can be terminated also by dispensation.

3. Suggested Norm

In specifying the duration of the time, it is well for the Ordinary to weigh the gravity of the crime, and time the suspension accordingly.[20] As to how great a time is just, is a matter which cannot easily be determined, and which in practice must be left to the judgment of the Ordinary. The Ordinary should take into consideration

[16] Cf. De Meester, *Compendium,* III_2, 1681.

[17] Cf. Santi-Leitner, *Praelectiones Juris Canonici,* V, 8; Arndt, "Die Suspension Ex Informata Conscientia,"—*AKKR,* 73 (1895), 164; Bourret, *Des Sentences,* p. 106.

[18] Cf. Instr. S. C. de P. F.,—*Collectanea,* n. 1628.

[19] *"Censura praecipue fertur ad reprimandam contumacian, et ut homo a culpa recedat, ideoque non potest alium terminum habere nisi dum recedat ab illa."*—Suarez, *De Censuris,* Disp. XXV, Sect. 1.—Arndt, "Die Suspension Ex Informata Conscientia,"—*AKKR,* 73 (1895), 164.

[20] Cf. Bassibey, "Des Sentences Ex Informata Conscientia,"—*JJC,* II (1893), 325.

the nature of the crime, and the circumstances in which it was committed; the previous reputation of the cleric; his character and qualities and present dispositions; beyond these general characteristics, there may be many extrinsic circumstances influencing the case, and of all these circumstances the Ordinary is the proper judge. However in general it can be said that he should lean rather towards mildness than to the side of severity.[21] Suffice it to say that the Holy See, judging from the replies of the Sacred Congregation in the past, does not favor too extensive a duration, and a norm given by authors would ordinarily limit the suspension to six months as a maximum. If the desired effects can be accomplished by a penalty of shorter duration, e.g., a day, a week or a month, then the Ordinary should so restrict the time. However, if there should be serious scandal involved in the case, it may be necessary to impose the penalty for a longer period. But even in this latter case, ordinarily the Ordinary should not go beyond the limit of six months. The circumstances which would necessitate a longer duration will be so rare and exceptional that they will seldom exist. If, however, after serious deliberation, the Ordinary prudently judges that the case demands a longer duration, the Holy See will judge the conditions which influenced the Ordinary, and if the case warrants such a duration, the Holy See will undoubtedly approve the decree of the Ordinary.

Article II—Irregularity

Formerly canonists disputed as to whether irregularity was incurred if this suspension was violated. It was held by all that irregularity was incurred if the suspension *ex informata conscientia* was inflicted as a censure, while many maintained it was not incurred when the suspension was a vindictive penalty.[22] However as early as 1625 it was maintained that irregularity was incurred by the violation of a suspension *ex informata conscientia* and in the case decided no distinction was made between the suspension as a censure

[21] Peries, "Suspension Ex Informata Conscientia,"—*ER*, XV (1896), 20.

[22] Cf. Gasparri, *De Sacra Ordinatione*, I, 358; he gives the views on either side of the question. Cf. also Lega, *De Judiciis Ecclesiasticis*, III, n. 325; D'Annibale, *Summula Theologiae Moralis*, I, 386.

and as a vindictive penalty.[23] In more recent times no distinction was made between the vindictive penalty and the censure, and it was commonly held that in both cases, without distinction, the violation of the suspension induced irregularity.[24] The question was definitely settled by the Code in favor of the more common opinion,[25] and now irregularity is incurred *ex delicto* by the violation of the suspension, whether it be a vindictive penalty or a censure.[26] However it is well to remember that contrary to the former law, when only a recourse *in devolutivo* was permitted,[27] the present law allows a recourse *in suspensivo* from the suspension *ex informata conscientia* if it is a vindictive penalty, while only *in devolutivo* if the suspension is a censure.[28] Consequently the exercise of the power of orders from which a person is suspended would not induce irregularity, while the recourse from a vindictive penalty is pending. It is well likewise to remember that should the suspension be null, from any cause whatever, irregularity is not incurred for its violation.[29] If it is doubtful whether the suspension, inflicted as a censure, is invalid, even though it is foreseen that in all probability the Holy See will overrule the decree of the Ordinary, the suspension must be observed under penalty of irregularity, while the recourse is pending;[30] this

[23] S. C. C., *Sagonen.*, 21 iun. 1625—*Fontes*, n. 2442. Cf. also Benedict XIV, *De Synodo Dioecesana,* lib. XII, cap. 8, n. 5.

[24] Vecchiotti, *Institutiones Canonicae,* II, 241; Santi-Leitner, *Praelectiones Juris Canonici,* V, 7; Devoti, *Institutionum Canonicarum,* II, 363; S. C. C., *Lucionen.*, 2 apr. 1848—*ASS,* XIV, 310; Suarez, *De Remotione Parochorum,* p. 238.

[25] Cf. Ferreres, *Institutiones Canonicae,* II, n. 936; Vermeersch-Creusen, *Epitome,* II, n. 257.

[26] C. 985, 7°.

[27] *"Recursus ipse non suspendit virtutem decreti episcopalis."* Santi-Leitner, *Praelectiones Juris Canonici,* V, 7. Cf. also Bassibey, "Des Sentences Ex Informata Conscientia,"—*JJC,* II (1893), 833.

[28] Cf. C. 2287 and C. 2243, § 1.

[29] Cf. Vering, *Droit Canon,* II, 450; Heiner, *Katholisches Kirchenrecht,* 45; Arndt, "Die Suspension Ex Informata Conscientia,"—*AKKR,* 73 (1895), 164.

[30] Cf. Bassibey, "Des Sentences Ex Informata Conscientia,"—*JJC,* II (1893), 833.

applies of course only to the recourse from the suspension as a censure and not to the suspension as a vindictive penalty, because in the latter case, the recourse is *in suspensivo,* and the effect of the suspension is not operative pending the decision of the case by the Holy See.

Article III—Solution of the Suspension

After a suspension *ex informata conscientia* has been inflicted, the cleric has the right to have recourse to the Holy See. If the Holy See nullifies the decree, the suspension does not bind the cleric. But if the Holy See approves the decree, or if no recourse is had, the suspension *ex informata conscientia* ceases according to the general norms laid down for the cessation of penalties in the Fifth Book of the Code, and these norms are different according as the suspension is a censure or a vindictive penalty.

If it is a censure, it can cease only by legitimate absolution.[31] In order that absolution be given, it is necessary that the suspended person recede from his contumacy;[32] but if he does recede from his contumacy, the Ordinary is obliged *ex justitia* to absolve him.[33] The right to judge whether the guilty cleric has in reality receded from his contumacy, belongs to him, from whom the absolution is asked,[34] provided of course this person has the power to absolve from the censure. Since the suspension *ex informata conscientia* is an *ab homine* censure,[35] it is reserved to the person who inflicted it, or to his superior,[36] successor or delegate;[37] and cannot be absolved by any other, even outside the territory of the Ordinary who inflicted it;[38] however those enumerated above have the power of absolving from the suspension, even though the guilty person transferred his domicile or quasidomicile elsewhere.[39] Since this is a censure which

[31] C. 2248. Cf. Cappello, *De Censuris,* p. 81-133.

[32] CC. 2242, 2248.

[33] Cf. Ayrinhac, *Penal Legislation,* p. 98.

[34] C. 2242, § 3.

[35] C. 2217, § 1, 3°.

[36] The superior here is the Holy See; in the case of religious, if the Provincial Superior imposed the suspension, the Superior General could likewise absolve from it.

[37] C. 2245, § 2.

[38] C. 2247, § 2.

[39] C. 2253, 2°.

does not impede the reception of the Sacraments, the sin for which the suspension is inflicted is not reserved and can be absolved by any confessor without special faculties.[40]

If it is a vindictive penalty, it can cease in two ways, either by expiation or by dispensation. It ceases by expiation, without any act of the superior, by the lapse of the time for which it was inflicted.[41] It ceases by dispensation, which can be given by him who has inflicted it, or by his superior, successor, or by one to whom this power has been delegated.[42] If however the suspension *ex informata conscientia* was inflicted *ad beneplacitum nostrum,* it ceases *ipso facto* with the resolution of the power of the person inflicting it, whether this power be lost by resignation, removal, transfer or death; such a suspension may also cease by dispensation.

Article IV—Substitute

Canon 2189. § 1. Si clericus suspensus sit ab officio in quo alius in eius locum substituendus est, ut, ex. gr., oeconomus in cura animarum, qui substituitur mercedem ex fructibus beneficii percipiat secundum prudens Ordinarii iudicium determinandam.

§ 2. Clericus suspensus, si se gravatum senserit, potest imminutionem pensionis ab immediato Superiore qui in via iudiciaria esset iudex appellationis.

The canon is concerned with a very practical point, and may arise in many cases of suspension *ex informata conscientia.* Since it will frequently be necessary to secure a substitute for the duration of the suspension, provision is made for the sustenance of the substitute. If this provision is too detrimental to the suspended cleric, the Code gives him the right of recourse.

A not infrequent result of the suspension *ex informata conscientia* will be the omission of certain ministrations which cannot be performed by the suspended cleric, and which nevertheless cannot be

[40] CC. 2250, § 1, 2246, § 3. Cf. Cappello, *De Censuris,* p. 100.

[41] Cf. Ayrinhac, *Penal Legislation,* 153.

[42] C. 2236, § 1. Cf. also C. 2290, § 1 for urgent cases.

omitted without a detriment to souls. Thus if a pastor is suspended from his office or from hearing confessions, it will be necessary to have a substitute appointed to take care of the parish, or to hear confessions, or to perform any other spiritual ministrations as the case may be, so that the regular pastoral care of souls will be in no way impeded.[43] The substitute must be supported, and since he is taking the place of the suspended cleric, it is but proper that he should receive his support from the benefice of the suspended cleric. Just how much he is to receive is a matter left to the prudent judgment of the Ordinary. It should not be the total income of the benefice or the total salary, because the suspended cleric does not lose his benefice, nor does he lose his right to receive the fruits thereof.[44] Although suspended, he still has a right to the sustenance proper to his station in life. The Ordinary is therefore to determine what portion the suspended cleric pay to the substitute, and the remainder belongs to the suspended cleric.

It may easily happen that either one or the other of the two will not be satisfied with the amount determined by the Ordinary. This canon makes no provision for the case when the substitute is dissatisfied; however he would have the right to submit his objection to the Ordinary, or perhaps even to seek an *actio jurium* to decide the matter. However the second paragraph of the canon explicitly states that the suspended cleric has a right of recourse if he feels that the judgment of the Ordinary is too burdensome for him. Since the determination of the Ordinary concerning the amount is not a judicial sentence, there can be no appeal in the proper sense; the same purpose however is obtained by recourse. Recourse in this case, contrary to that allowed against the suspension itself, is to be had to the superior, who, if it were a judicial matter, would be the judge of the second instance.[45] If the Ordinary inflicting the censure is a suffragan bishop, recourse is had to the metropolitan court of appeal.[46] If the recourse is from an Arch-

[43] C. 472. Cf. Blat, *Commenatrium,* IV, n. 796.

[44] It has been shown in a previous chapter that the power to suspend *ex informata conscientia* does not extend to a suspension from a benefice.

[45] No special formula is required. In presenting his petition to the Metropolitan Court, the cleric should mention canon 2189.

[46] C. 1594, § 1.

bishop, it is to be had to the diocese or archdiocese, which the Archbishop has chosen with the approbation of the Holy See, *semel pro semper,* to be the court of second instance for his archdiocese.[47] If the recourse is from an Archbishop lacking suffragans, or from an Ordinary immediately subject to the Holy See, it is to the closer metropolitan see, which has been chosen with the previous approbation of the Holy See, *semel pro semper* to receive appeals.[48] If the recourse is from a religious Ordinary, the recourse is placed in the hands of the person, who according to the Constitutions, constitutes the court of the second instance; e.g., from a Provincial Superior to the Superior General.[49]

Article V—Recourse

Canon 2194. Si clericus recursum a suspensione sibi inflicta interponat, Ordinarius ad Sedem Apostolicam mittere debet probationes quibus constet clericum delictum revera perpetrasse quod extraordinaria hac poena puniri queat.

In connection with the other questions treated above, it has been necessary to make frequent mention of the right of recourse which a suspended cleric has against a suspension *ex informata conscientia.* Although this right is not expressly given to him by canon 2194, it is assumed that he has it, because the canon states that if the cleric has recourse, the Ordinary must forward the proofs to the Holy See. This right is explicitly given the cleric in canon 2146, but even were it not explicitly given, the cleric would none the less have the right. In a hierarchical form of government, the actions of an inferior, exercising subordinate jurisdiction, are always subject to the review of the superior. In the government of the Church there is a well graduated hierarchical order, with one supreme Superior, the Roman Pontiff. In ordinary judicial matters, a person who feels that justice has not been rendered to him by his Ordinary, can appeal his case to the Metropolitan, and further can appeal from the Metropolitan to the Holy See. The definite determination of the court of second

[47] C. 1594, § 2.

[48] C. 285, c. 1594, § 3.

[49] C. 1594, § 4; c. 1579; cf. Ferreres, *Institutiones Canonicae,* II, n. 551.

instance, together with a precise delineation of the conditions and rights of appeal, of course must be determined by ecclesiastical law, but the fundamental right of a subject to take his case from an immediate superior to a higher superior is based upon the very nature of a hierarchical institution.[50]

The right of appeal in the strict sense of that term is not permitted to a cleric who has been suspended *ex informata conscientia.* This has been the law from its very inception in the Council of Trent,[51] and the Sacred Congregations have frequently expressly stated this.[52] The present law upholds the old law. An appeal may be taken only from a judicial sentence and since the suspension *ex informata conscientia* is not imposed by a judicial sentence, it is not possible to appeal from it. However the cleric is not left without a remedy of law, and this remedy is recourse to the Holy See. This right of recourse, as has been said, is based upon the very nature of a hierarchical institution, and its application in the case of the suspension *ex informata conscientia* has always been expressly recognized by the Holy See, which has shown itself prompt in accepting any cases presented to it.

When appeals are made to the Holy See, they are considered by the Rota, the appellate tribunal of the Holy See. However this is not the case with recourse. The right to handle the recourse made to the Holy See from the decrees of Ordinaries is the exclusive province of the Sacred Congregations.[53] Which particular congregation will handle any definite recourse, depends upon the nature of the particular case. Recourse from the decree of the suspension *ex informata conscientia* is within the competence of the following Congregations:

[50] Cf. Arndt, "Die Suspension Ex Informata Conscientia,"—*AKKR,* 73 (1895), 166; Bassibey, "Des Sentences Ex Informata Conscientia,"—*JJC,* II (1893), 706.

[51] *". . . nulla contra ipsius praelati voluntatem concessa licentia de se promoveri faciendo aut ad priores ordines, gradus, dignitates sive honores restitutio suffragetur."*—Conc. Trid., Sess. XIV, cap. 1, de reform.

[52] S. C. C., *Sagonen.,* 21 iun. 1623—*Fontes,* n. 2442; S. C. C., *Bononien.,* 14 nov. 1654—*Fontes,* n. 2741; Instr. S. C. de P. F., 10 oct. 1884,—*Collectanea,* n. 1628.

[53] C. 1601.

a) The Sacred Congregation of the Council is competent in the recourse of secular clerics against a suspension *ex informata conscientia* by their Ordinaries.

b) The Sacred Congregation of Religious is competent if the recourse is had by a religious against his religious superior or against the Local Ordinary.

c) The Sacred Congregation of the Propagation of the Faith is competent to receive the recourse of clerics living in places which are subject to this Congregation.

d) The Sacred Congregation of Orientals is competent in the case of Orientals.

e) The Holy Office is competent if the recourse is concerned with questions in which it has sole competence.

Should a doubt arise as to which congregation is competent in a particular case, the recourse may be sent to the Secretary of State, and he will forward it to the proper and competent Congregation. In applying for this recourse, no special formula is required.

The effect of the recourse depends upon the nature of the suspension *ex informata conscientia,* and is different according as the suspension is a censure or a vindictive penalty. Before the Code a recourse from a suspension *ex informata conscientia* followed the general rules of recourse, and was always *in devolutivo* only; in other words, pending the recourse the cleric was bound to abide by the suspension *ex informata conscientia,* and its violation caused irregularity at least in the case of the censure; while it was held by some that no irregularity was incurred by the violation if the suspension was a vindictive penalty.[64] Some authors, seemingly unmindful of the Code legislation still hold that a recourse from a suspension *ex informata conscientia,* whether this be a censure or vindictive penalty, is possible only *in devolutivo.*[65] However the general norms of the Fifth Book of the Code apply also to the suspension *ex informata conscientia,* and consequently must be followed

[64] Cf. Rivet, *Institutiones Iuris Ecclesiastici Privati,* II, 115.

[65] Cf. Wernz-Vidal, *Jus Canonicum,* VI, n. 805; Blat, *Commentarium,* IV, n. 807; Bouuaert-Simenon, *Manuale,* n. 1237; Ferreres, *Institutiones Canonicae,* II, n. 940; Augustine, *Commentary,* VII, 482; De Meester, *Compendium,* III_2, n. 1695.

in this matter. Accordingly when the suspension *ex informata conscientia* is a censure, recourse from it is possible only *in devolutivo;*[56] therefore, notwithstanding the recourse, the censure must be observed until the Holy See settles the case. On the other hand, if the suspension *ex informata conscientia* is a vindictive penalty, recourse from it is *in suspensivo,* i.e., pending the recourse the suspension is suspended and need not be observed. *"Ab inflictis poenis vindicativis datur appellatio seu recursus in suspensivo, nisi aliud expresse in iure caveatur."* [57] Nowhere is the contrary expressly stated with regard to the suspension *ex informata conscientia,* and consequently there is no doubt but that the recourse from a vindictive penalty of suspension *ex informata conscientia* is *in suspensivo.*[58]

Since, according to canon 2287, a recourse from a vindictive penalty is *in suspensivo,* the question immediately arises as to whether this recourse is affected by the *fatalia legis.* In Canon 2194 no time limit is given for having the recourse. This offers no difficulty in the case of the suspension as a censure, because in this case the recourse is only *in devolutivo* and follows the general norm of recourse. In general a resource may be made at any time and is not subject to the *fatalia legis.* This is evident from the nature of the case. The *fatalia,* a specified time limit granted for appeal or recourse, bind the judge or superior, even as they bind the party, who institutes the appeal or recourse. But in the suspension *ex informata conscientia,* the recourse is to the Holy See, and it is wrong to say that the Holy See is bound to a certain time limit in receiving a recourse. All are free to approach the Holy See at any time. Consequently in the case when the suspension *ex informata conscientia* is a censure, the decree of suspension takes immediate effect, needing no execution, and the suspended person is bound to abide by the suspension, even though he have recourse to the Holy See. In this case therefore there is no necessity to set a time limit to the recourse, but at any time during the suspension, he could apply to the Holy

[56] C. 2243, § 1.

[57] C. 2287.

[58] Cf. Muniz, *Procedimientos Eclesiasticos,* I, n. 718; Suarez,—*De Remotione Parochorum,* p. 214.

See for settlement; but until an answer were received from the Holy See, he would certainly be bound to observe the censure.

Is this same norm to be applied to the suspension *ex informata conscientia* as a vindictive penalty? On the one hand, the liberty of the person to have recourse to the Holy See must be safeguarded, but on the other hand, if no limit is placed to the right of the cleric to interpose his recourse, it can easily be seen that disastrous consequences would result. Since the recourse in the case is *in suspensivo,* the effects of the suspension do not operate, pending the recourse. If a cleric would therefore wait a long time to make this recourse, it is evident that the ends of justice are being frustrated and the jurisdiction of the Ordinary is being impeded. It is not the wish of the Church that justice be interfered with by dilatory measures of this kind. In view of this, it seems but just that a definite limit should be set to the time allowed for suspensive recourse, and since a definite norm is not given in canon 2194, canon 20 must be applied and a norm sought from laws for similar cases.

The general norm of the Code for appeals has a restrictive time limit. A person loses his right of appeal if he does not appeal within ten days of the notice of the publication of the judicial sentence.[60] From judicial sentences appeals are ordinarily granted *in suspensivo*. The similarity of the case of appeals *in suspensivo* to the recourse *in suspensivo* from a vindictive penalty of suspension *ex informata conscientia* is apparent. That an authoritative argument may be drawn in favor of applying the legislation on appeals to the case of the recourse in question appears more strikingly, when one studies the replies of the Sacred Congregations on similar questions.

From the definitive decree of removal a pastor has a right to have recourse to the Holy See. Canon 2146 specifies that if the pastor interposes this recourse, the Ordinary cannot validly confer the parish or benefice permanently on anyone else, while the recourse is pending. In this canon there is no time limit set, during which the recourse must be made, and since the power of the Ordinary is impeded in making permanent assignments pending the recourse, it is evident to what inconvenience a complete lack of a time limit would lead. But since no specific law covered the case, the Holy See was peti-

[60] C. 1881.

tioned to give a decision on the question. The Sacred Congregation applied the law on appeals to the case in question, and decided that the *fatalia legis* did apply, and consequently that recourse from such a definitive decree, to obtain the effect of canon 2146, § 3, had to be interposed within ten days *(tempus utile)*.[60]

A similar decision was handed down by the Sacred Congregation of Religious. Canon 647, § 2, 4° grants a religious the right to have recourse to the Holy See against the decree of dismissal, and this recourse is *in suspensivo*, because the canon clearly states that pending the recourse, the dismissal has no juridical effect. Here again there is nothing in the canon which applies the *fatalia legis* to this recourse; but, unless they are applied, serious inconveniences would result, and the jurisdiction of the religious superiors who insued the decree of dismissal would be seriously hampered. When the case was presented to the Holy See, the Sacred Congregation applied the time limit of ten days also to this case.[61] This latter decision is very important because of its exact wording. The Sacred Congregation said that the time allowed for having the recourse is ten days, in as far as the suspensive effect is concerned. Consequently it upholds the right of the religious to have recourse to the Holy See at any time, but if that recourse is to have suspensive effect, it must be made within ten days. Further the Sacred Congregation explicitly states that this decision is based upon the law decreed for similar cases.

In view of these decisions, it seems reasonable to conclude that the same norm must be followed in regard to the suspension *ex informata conscientia* as a vindictive penalty. The recourse here is *in suspensivo* and if no time limit is set, the jurisdiction of the Ordinary is hampered, and a cleric could frustrate the application of a just penalty to himself. Therefore it seems proper to apply the same norm concerning the *fatalia legis* to this recourse, and to limit it in its suspensive effects to ten days. This time is *tempus utile* and does not lapse if a person is ignorant of the penalty, or unable to have the recourse, e.g., because of a serious illness. The time begins when the cleric receives the notice of the suspension, and is to be reckoned according to canon 34, § 3, 3°. Consequently the first day is not

[60] S. C. C., *Romana et aliarum*, 12 ian. 1924—*AAS*, XVI (1924), 162.

[61] S. C. Rel., 20 iul. 1923—*AAS*, XV (1923), 457.

counted, and the time lasts until ten complete days have lapsed, e.g., if a cleric received the decree on April 1, he would be allowed to interpose his recourse with suspensive effect until midnight on April 11. If he does not have the recourse during this period, the suspensive effect of the recourse ceases, and the suspension is operative. However any time thereafter he could still place his case before the Holy See, but in this case the recourse would be only *in devolutivo*.

Canon 2194 expressly requires the Ordinary to forward the proofs to the Holy See. If the cleric interposes a recourse from the suspension inflicted on him, the Ordinary must send to the Holy See, the proofs by which it is evident that the cleric really perpetrated a crime which can be punished by this extraordinary penalty. This disposition of the law is distinctly favorable to the suspended cleric. He simply places his case before the Holy See, and is not required to prove his innocence. The burden of proof rests entirely with the Ordinary, who, immediately upon the announcement of the cleric that he has availed himself of his right of recourse, should forward the proofs to the Holy See.[62]

From this canon, even as from the earlier canons, dealing with the collection of the proofs, it is clear that Ordinary must prove three things: in the first place that the cleric really committed the crime for which he is punished; secondly that the crime is sufficiently grave and of such a nature to merit so drastic a punishment; and thirdly that it was impossible for the Ordinary to have proceeded in the case against the cleric according to the ordinary norms of law.[63]

It will not be superfluous to remark that the Holy See scrutinizes these proofs very closely and is inclined to favor the suspended cleric.[64] As has been pointed out in the first part of this work, the history of the Sacred Congregation affords numerous instances where the suspensions have not been upheld. Some of the more common

[62] Cf. Muniz, *Procedimientos Eclesiasticos,* I, n. 718; Augustine, *Commentary,* VII, 483.

[63] CC. 2186, 2190, 2194; cf. Suarez, *De Remotione Parochorum,* p. 261.

[64] Cf. "Des Sentences Ex Informata Conscientia,"—*JJC,* II (1893), 707. *"Suspensi ex informata conscientia reperiunt nedum humanissimos judices, sed juriumque cujusque integerrimos propugnatores."*—Pallottini, *Pugna Juris Pontificii,* 116.

causes for which such suspensions have been overruled are: lack of competence; injustice of the suspension; excessiveness of the penalty, either in itself, its duration or other circumstances; lack of the necessary formalities.[65] If the Ordinaries could not sufficiently prove their case, the Holy See has not been slow in repudiating their decisions.[66] In these cases, the Ordinary is held to reparation and must bear the expenses; he must make restitution especially with regards to the fruits of the benefice.[67]

[65] Cf. Bassibey, "Des Sentences Ex Informata Conscientia,"—*JJC,* II (1893), 709; Arndt, "Die Suspension Ex Informata Conscientia,"—*AKKR,* 73 (1895), 166; Cocchi, *Commentarium,* IV, 647.

[66] Cf. Wernz-Vidal, *Jus Canonicum,* VI, n. 805.

[67] S. C. C., *S. Severini,* 19 sept. 1778,—*Thesaurus Resolutionum,* XLVII, 47; Pallottini, *Pugna Juris Pontificii,* 116; Arndt, "Die Suspension Ex Informata Conscientia,"—*AKKR,* 73 (1895), 165; Vermeersch-Creusen, *Epitome,* III, n. 381; Suarez, *De Remotione Parochorum,* p. 261.

BIBLIOGRAPHY

Sources

Acta Apostolicae Sedis, Romae, 1909—

Acta Sanctae Sedis, 41 vols., Romae, 1865-1908.

Bullarii Romani Continuatio Summorum Pontificum, 19 vols., Prati, 1765-1883.

Canones et Decreta Concilii Tridentini, Taurini, 1913.

Codex Juris Canonici Pii X Pontificis Maximi jussu digestus Benedicti Papae XV auctoritate promulgatus, Romae, 1930.

Codicis Juris Canonici Fontes cura Emi Petri Card. Gasparri editi, 5 vols., Romae, 1923-1930.

Collectanea in Usum Secretariae S. C. Episcoporum et Regularium, Bizzarri, Romae, 1885.

Collectanea Sacrae Congregationis de Propaganda Fide, 2 vols., Romae, 1907.

Corpus Juris Canonici, Editio Lipsiensis II (Richter-Friedberg), 2 vols., Lipsiae, 1922.

Mansi, Joannes Dominicus, *Sacrorum Conciliorum Nova et Amplissima Collectio,* 53 vols., Paris, 1901-1919.

Thesaurus Resolutionum Sacrae Congregationis Concilii, 167 vols., Romae, 1718-1908.

Waterworth, J., *The Canons and Decrees of the Council of Trent,* London, 1848.

Reference Works

Arndt, Augustin, *Die Suspension "Ex Informata Conscientia"*—AKKR, 73 (1895), 141-170.

[Bachofen], Charles Augustine, *A Commentary on the New Code of Canon Law,* 8 vols., St. Louis, 1921-25.

Ayrinhac, H. A., *Penal Legislation,* New York, 1920.

Barbosa, Augustinus, *Collectanea in Jus Pontificium Universum,* Lugduni, 1646.

Bareille, Georges, *Code du Droit Canonique,* Arras, 1920.

Bassibey, R., *Des Sentences "Ex Informata Conscientia"*—JJC (1893).

Benedictus XIV, *De Synodo Dioecesana,* 2 vols., Romae, 1806.

Bevilacqua, Americo, *De Episcopi seu Ordinarii Juribus ac Obligationibus,* Romae, 1921.

Blat, Alberto, *Commentarium Textus Codicis Canonici,* 6 vols., Romae, 1921-27.

Boriero, Franciscus, *Manuale Processo Canonico,* Padova, 1909.

Bouix, D., *De Judiciis Ecclesiasticis,* 2 ed., 2 vols., Paris, 1866.

Bourret, Francois, *Des Sentences ecclésiastiques,* Montpellier, 1909.

Cance, Adrien, *Le Code de Droit Canonique,* 3 vols., Paris, 1929.

Cappello, Felix M., *Tractatus Canonico-Moralis De Censuris,* 3 ed., Taurini, 1925.

Cavagnis, Felix, *Institutiones Juris Publici Ecclesiastici*, 2 ed., 2 vols., Romae, 1889.

Claeys-Bouuaert, F., *De Canonica Cleri Saecularis Obedientia*, Louvanii, 1904.

Claeys-Bouuaert-Simenon, *Manuale Juris Canonici*, 2 ed., Bandae et Leodii, 1926.

Cocchi, Guidus, *Commentarium in Codicem Juris Canonici ad Usum Scholarum, Liber IV De Processibus*, Taurinorum Augustae, 1930.

D'Annibale, I., *Summula Theologiae Moralis*, Romae, 3 vols., 1908.

De Angelis, Philippus, *Praelectiones Juris Canonici*, 3 vols., Romae, 1877-78.

De Luca, Marianus, *Praelectiones Juris Canonici*, 3 vols., Romae, 1897.

De Luca, Joannis B., *Theatrum Veritatis et Justitiae*, 16 vols., Coloniae Agrippinae, 1706.

De Meester, A., *Juris Canonici et Juris Canonici-Civilis Compendium*, 3 vols., Brugis, 1921-28.

Devoti, Joannes, *Institutionum Canonicarum, Libri IV*, Leodii, 1883.

Droste-Messmer, A., *Canonical Procedure*, New York, 1887.

Fagnanus, Prosperus, *Commentaria in V Libros Decretalium*, Venetiis, 1696.

Falco, Maria, *Codex Juris Canonici*, Torino, 1925.

Ferraris, Lucius, *Bibliotheca Prompta Canonica, Juridica, Moralis, Theologica*, 9 vols., Romae, 1885—

Ferreres, Joannes B., *Institutiones Canonicae*, 2 vols., Barcinone, 1920.

Gallemart, Joannes, *Concilium Tridentinum*, Tridenti, 1737.

Gasparri, Petro, *Tractatus Canonicus De Sacra Ordinatione*, 2 vols., Paris, 1893.

Giraldi, Ubaldus, *Expositio Juris Pontificii*, 2 vols., Romae, 1829.

Gennari, *Sulla Privazione del beneficio ecclesiastico*, Romae, 1905.

Gongalez, Emanuel, Tellez, *Commentaria Perpetua Decretalium*, 4 vols., Lugduni, 1715.

Haring, Johann B., *Grundzüge des Katholischen Kirchenrechts*, 2 vols., Graz., 1924.

Heiner, Franz, *Katholisches Kirchenrecht*, 2 vols., Paderborn, 1909.

Hergenröther, Philipp, *Lehrbuch des Katholischen Kirchenrechts*, Freiburg in Breisgau, 1888.

Hinschius, Paul, *System des Katholischen Kirchenrechts*, 6 vols., Berlin, 1869-1895.

Kober, F., *Die Suspension*, Tuebingen, 1862.

Laemmer, Hugo, *Institutionen des Katholischen Kirchenrechts*, Freiburg in Breisgau, 1892.

Lega, Michael, *De Judiciis Ecclesiasticis*, 4 vols., Romae, 1898.

Leurenius, Petrus, *Forum Ecclesiasticum de Universo Jure Canonico*, 5 vols., Venetiis, 1729.

Lombardi, Carolus, *Juris Canonici Privati Institutiones*, 2 ed., 3 vols., Romae, 1901.

Makee, Ch., *Institutiones Juris Ecclesiastici*, 2 vols., Romae, 1897.

Manacorda, Aemilianus, *Specimen Juris et Disciplinae Ecclesiasticae,* 2 vols., Fossani, 1897.
Molitor, Raphael, *Religiosi Juris Capita Selecta,* New York, 1909.
Molitor, Wilhelm, *Kanonisches Gerichtsverfahren,* Mainz, 1836.
Mothon, Joseph Pie, *Institutions Canoniques,* 3 vols., Paris, 1922.
Muniz, T., *Procedimientos Eclesiasticos,* 3 vols., Seville, 1930.
Noval, Josepho, "De Ratione Corrigendi,"—*Jus Pontificium,* II (1922).
Noval, Josepho, *Commentarium Codicis Canonici, Liber IV De Processibus,* Romae, 1920.
Pallavicini, Sforza, *Istoria del Concilio di Trento,* 4 vols., Romae, 1833.
Pallottini, S., *Collectio Omnium Conclusionum et Resolutionum . . . S. Congregationis S. Concilii Tridentini, 1564-1860,* 17 vols., Romae, 1868-1893.
Pallottini, S., *Pugna Juris Pontificii Statuentis Suspensiones, etc.,* Viennae, 1863.
Palmieri, Dominicus, "Vis Particulae ETIAM in c. 1, Sess. XIV Conc. Trid. de Reform."—*Analecta Ecclesiastica,* II (1894).
Pejska, Josephus, *Jus Canonicum Religiosorum,* Friburgi Brisgoviae, 1928.
Pelella, Josephus, *Canones et Decreta Concilii Tridentini,* Neapoli, 1859.
Peries, G., *La Procédure Canonique,* Paris, 1898.
Peries, G., *Suspension Ex Informata Conscientia,—ER,* XV (1896).
Pierantonelli, Jacobus, *Praxis Fori Ecclesiastici,* Romae, 1883.
Pignatelli, Jacobus, *Consultationes Canonicae,* 11 vols., Coloniae Allobrogum, 1700.
Pirhing, Enricus, *Jus Canonicum in V Libros Decretalium,* 4 vols., Dilingae, 1674-78.
R. de M., *Institutiones Juris Canonici,* Paris, 1853.
Richter, *Kirchenrecht,* 2 vols., 1882-1886.
Rights of the Clergy Vindicated, New York, 1883.
Rivet, L., *Institutiones Juris Ecclesiastici Privati,* 2 vols., Romae, 1914.
Roberti, Francisco, *De Processibus,* 2 vols., Romae, 1926.
Santi, F.-Leitner, M., *Praelectiones Juris Canonici,* 4 ed., 5 vols., Romae, 1904.
Schmier, Franciscus, *Jurisprudentia Canonico-Civilis,* 2 vols., Venetiis, 1754.
Smith, S. B., *Elements of Ecclesiastical Law,* New York, 2 vols., 1882.
Smith, S. B., *The New Procedure in Criminal and Disciplinary Cases,* New York, 1898.
Sole, Jacobus, *De Delictis et Poenis,* Romae, 1920.
Suarez, Emmanuele, *De Remotione Parochorum,* Romae, 1931.
Van Espen, Z. Bernardus, *Jus Ecclesiasticum Universum,* 5 vols., Louvanii, 1753.
Vecchiotti, Septimus, *Institutiones Canonicae,* 3 vols., Taurinorum Augustae, 1886.
Vering, Fred.,-Belet, P., *Droit Canon,* 2 vols., Paris, 1881.
Vermeersch-Creusen, *Epitome Juris Canonici,* 3 vols., Brugis, 1928.
Vidal, Petrus, "Notio Delicti in Jure Codicis,"—*Jus Pont.,* I (1921).
Wernz, Franciscus, *Jus Decretalium,* 6 vols., Romae, 1906-1913.

Wernz-Vidal, *Jus Canonicum*, Vol. VI: *De Processibus*, Romae, 1928.
Zitelli, Zephyrinus, *Apparatus Juris Ecclesiastici*, Romae, 1886.

PERIODICALS

American Ecclesiastical Review, The (ER), Philadelphia, 1889—
Analecta Ecclesiastica, Romae, 1893-1911.
Analecta Juris Pontificii, Romae, 1855-68; Paris, 1869-90.
Archiv für katholisches Kirchenrecht (AKKR), Mainz, 1857—
Irish Ecclesiastical Record, The, Dublin, 1864—
Journal du Droit Canon et de la Jurisprudence Canonique (JJC), Paris, 1880-1894.
Jus Pontificium (Jus Pont.), Romae, 1921—

Universitas Catholica Americae

WASHINGTON, D. C.

FACULTAS JURIS CANONICI

No. 76

1932

DEUS LUX MEA

TITULI

QUOS

AD DOCTORATUS GRADUM

IN

JURE CANONICO

APUD UNIVERSITATEM CATHOLICAM AMERICAE

CONSEQUENDUM

PUBLICE PROPUGNABIT

EDUINUS JACOBUS MURPHY

SACERDOS CONGREGATIONIS PRETIOSISSIMI SANGUINIS

JURIS CANONICI LICENTIATUS

HORA XI, A. M., DIE XXI MAII MCMXXXII

TITULI

IN IURE CANONICO

I.	De Dissertatione.	
II.	De Iuris Canonici Historia.	
III.	Canones 1-7	De Ambitu Codicis.
IV.	Canones 8-24	De Legibus Ecclesiasticis.
V.	Canones 25-30	De Consuetudine.
VI.	Canones 31-35	De Temporis Supputatione.
VII.	Canones 36-62	De Rescriptis.
VIII.	Canones 118-123	De Iuribus et Privilegiis Clericorum.
IX.	Canones 492-498	De Erectione et Suppressione Religionis, Provinciae, Domus.
X.	Canones 499-517	De Superioribus et de Capitulis.
XI.	Canones 518-530	De Confessariis et de Cappellanis.
XII.	Canones 531-537	De Bonis Temporalibus Eorumque Administratione.
XIII.	Canones 539-541	De Postulatu.
XIV.	Canones 542-552	De Requisitis ut Quis in Novitiatum Admitatur.
XV.	Canones 553-571	De Novitiorum Institutione.
XVI.	Canones 572-586	De Professione Religiosa.
XVII.	Canones 587-591	De Ratione Studiorum in Religionibus Clericalibus.
XVIII.	Canones 592-612	De Obligationibus Religiosorum.
XIX.	Canones 613-625	De Privilegiis Religiosorum.
XX.	Canones 737-779	De Baptismo.
XXI.	Canones 1012-1018	De Matrimonio in Genere.
XXII.	Canones 1058-1066	De Impedimentis Impedientibus.
XXIII.	Canones 1067-1080	De Impedimentis Dirimentibus.
XXIV.	Canones 1094-1103	De Forma Celebrationis Matrimonii.
XXV.	Canones 1104-1107	De Matrimonio Conscientiae.
XXVI.	Canones 1406-1408	De Fidei Professione.
XXVII.	Canones 1552-1568	De Notione Iudicii et De Foro Competenti.
XXVIII.	Canones 1572-1593	De Tribunali Ordinario Primae Instantiae.
XXIX.	Canones 1608-1645	De Disciplina in Tribunalibus Servanda.
XXX.	Canones 1646-1666	De Partibus in Causa.
XXXI.	Canones 1706-1725	De Causae Introductione.
XXXII.	Canones 1726-1731	De Litis Instantia.
XXXIII.	Canones 1750-1753	De Confessione Partium.
XXXIV.	Canones 1770-1781	De Examine Testium.
XXXV.	Canones 1812-1824	De Probatione per Instrumenta.
XXXVI.	Canones 2162-2167	De Translatione Parochorum.
XXXVII.	Canones 2195-2198	De Natura Delicti.

XXXVIII. Canones 2214-2220 De Poenis in Genere.
XXXIX. Canones 2241-2285 De Censuris.
XL. Canones 2306-2311 De Poenalibus Remediis.
XLI. The Periods of Roman Law.
XLII. The Sources of Roman Law.
XLIII. Personality.
XLIV. Slavery.
XLV. Citizenship.
XLVI. Patria Potestas.
XLVII. Personae in Manu.
XLVIII. Tutela et Cura.
XLIX. Personae in Mancipio.
L. Ownership.
LI. De Obligationibus in Genere.
LII. De Obligationibus Extra-Contractualibus.
LIII. Furtum.
LIV. Damnum Iniuria Datum.
LV. De Actionibus.

AMERICAN CHURCH—CIVIL LAW

LVI. Juridical Status of the Church in the United States.
LVII. Methods of Holding Church Property.
LVIII. Tax Exemption.
LIX. Marriage.
LX. Cemeteries.

Vidit Facultas:

VALENTINUS T. SCHAAF, O.F.M., J.C.D., Vice-Decanus.
LUDOVICUS H. MOTRY, S.T.D., J.C.D, a Secretis.
FRANCISCUS J. LARDONE, S.T.D., J.U.D.
JOHN McDILL FOX, A.B., LL.B.

Vidit Rector Magnificus Universitatis:

JACOBUS HUGO RYAN, S.T.D., PH.D., LL.D., LITT.D.

BIOGRAPHICAL NOTE

Edwin James Murphy was born in St. Joseph, Mo., August 11, 1905. After completing his elementary studies in St. Francis Xavier's School, he began his preparation for the priesthood with the Society of the Precious Blood. From 1918 to 1922 he attended St. Mary's Preparatory Seminary, Burkettsville, Ohio. December 3, 1923, he became a member of the Society. From 1922 to 1930 he attended St. Charles Seminary, Carthagena, Ohio, completing his junior college, philosophical and theological courses. He was ordained to the priesthood at Carthagena on May 3, 1930. In September, 1930, he began his graduate course in Canon Law at the Catholic University of America.

CANON LAW STUDIES

1. FRERIKS, REV. CELESTINE A., C.PP.S., J.C.D., Religious Congregations in Their External Relations, 121 pp., 1916.
2. GALLIHER, REV. DANIEL M., O.P., J.C.D., Canonical Elections, 117 pp., 1917.
3. BORKOWSKI, REV. AURELIUS L., O.F.M., De Confraternitatibus Ecclesiasticis, 136 pp., 1918.
4. CASTILLO, REV. CAYO, J.C.D., Disertacion Historico-canonica sobre la Potestad del Cabildo en Sede Vacante o Impedida del Vicario Capitular, 99 pp., 1919 (1918).
5. KUBELBECK, REV. WILLIAM J., S.T.B., J.C.D., The Sacred Penitentiaria and Its Relations to Faculties of Ordinaries and Priests, 129 pp., 1918.
6. PETROVITS, REV. JOSEPH J. C., S.T.D., J.C.D., The New Church Law on Matrimony, X-461 pp., 1919.
7. HICKEY, REV. JOHN J., S.T.B., J.C.D., Irregularities and Simple Impediments in the New Code of Canon Law, 100 pp., 1920.
8. KLEKOTKA, REV. PETER J., S.T.B., J.C.D., Diocesan Consultors, 179 pp., 1920.
9. WANNENMACHER, REV. FRANCIS, J.C.D., The Evidence in Ecclesiastical Procedure Affecting the Marriage Bond, 1920. (Not Printed.)
10. GOLDEN, REV. HENRY FRANCIS, J.C.D., Parochial Benefices in the New Code, IV-119 pp., 1921. (Printed 1925.)
11. KOUDELKA, REV. CHARLES J., J.C.D., Pastors, Their Rights and Duties According to the New Code of Canon Law, 211 pp., 1921.
12. MELO, REV. ANTONIUS, O.F.M., J.C.D., De Exemptione Regularium, X-188 pp., 1921.
13. SCHAAF, REV. VALENTINE THEODORE, O.F.M., S.T.B., J.C.D., The Cloister, X-180 pp., 1921.
14. BURKE, REV. THOMAS JOSEPH, S.T.B., J.C.D., Competence in Ecclesiastical Tribunals, IV-117 pp., 1922.
15. LEECH, REV. GEORGE LEO, J.C.D., A Comparative Study of the Constitution "Apostolicae Sedis" and the "Codex Juris Canonici," 179 pp., 1922.
16. MOTRY, REV. HUBERT LOUIS, S.T.D., J.C.D., Diocesan Faculties according to the Code of Canon Law, II-167 pp., 1922.
17. MURPHY, REV. GEORGE LAWRENCE, J.C.D., Delinquencies and Penalties in the Administration and the Reception of the Sacraments, IV-121 pp., 1923.
18. O'REILLY, REV. JOHN ANTHONY, S.T.B., J.C.D., Ecclesiastical Sepulture in the New Code of Canon Law, II-129 pp., 1923.
19. MICHALICKA, REV. WENCESLAS CYRILL, O.S.B., J.C.D., Judicial Procedure in Dismissal of Clerical Exempt Religious, 107 pp., 1923.
20. DARGIN, REV. EDWARD VINCENT, S.T.B., J.C.D., Reserved Cases According to the Code of Canon Law, IV-103 pp., 1924.
21. GODFREY, REV. JOHN A., S.T.B., J.C.D., The Right of Patronage According to the Code of Canon Law, 153 pp., 1924.
22. HAGEDORN, REV. FRANCIS EDWARD, J.C.D., General Legislation on Indulgences, II-154 pp., 1924.

23. King, Rev. James Ignatius, J.C.D., The Administration of the Sacraments to Dying Non-Catholics, V-141 pp., 1924.
24. Winslow, Rev. Francis Joseph, A.F.M., J.C.D., Vicars and Prefects Apostolic, IV-149 pp., 1924.
25. Correa, Rev. Jose Servelion, S.T.L., J.C.D., La Potestad Legislativa de la Iglesia Católica, IV-127 pp., 1925.
26. Dugan, Rev. Henry Francis, M.A., J.C.D., The Judiciary Department of the Diocesan Curia, 87 pp., 1925.
27. Keller, Rev. Charles Frederick, S.T.B., J.C.D., Mass Stipends, 167 pp., 1925.
28. Paschang, Rev. John Linus, J.C.D., The Sacramentals According to the Code of Canon Law, 129 pp., 1925.
29. Piontek, Rev. Cyrillus, O.F.M., S.T.B., J.C.D., De Indulto Exclaustrationis necnon Saecularizationis, XIII-289 pp., 1925.
30. Kearney, Rev. Richard Joseph, S.T.B., J.C.D., Sponsors at Baptism According to the Code of Canon Law, IV-127 pp., 1925.
31. Bartlett, Rev. Chester Joseph, A.M., LL.B., J.C.D., The Tenure of Parochial Property in the United States of America, V-108 pp., 1926.
32. Kilker, Rev. Adrian Jerome, J.C.D., Extreme Unction, V-425 pp., 1926.
33. McCormick, Rev. Robert Emmett, J.C.D., Confessors of Religious, VIII-266 pp., 1926.
34. Miller, Rev. Newton Thomas, J.C.D., Founded Masses According to the Code of Canon Law, VII-93 pp., 1926.
35. Roelker, Rev. Edward G., S.T.D., J.C.D., Principles of Privilege According to the Code of Canon Law, XI-166 pp., 1926.
36. Bakalarczyk, Rev. Richardus, M.I.C., J.U.D., De Novitiatu, VIII-208 pp., 1927.
37. Pizzuti, Rev. Lawrence, O.F.M., J.U.L., De Parochis Religiosis, 1927. (Not Printed.)
38. Bliley, Rev. Nicholas Martin, O.S.B., J.C.D., Altars According to the Code of Canon Law, XIX-132 pp., 1927.
39. Brown, Brendan Francis, A.B., LL.M., J.U.D., The Canonical Juristic Personality with Special Reference to its Status in the United States of America, V-212 pp., 1927.
40. Cavanaugh, Rev. William Thomas. C.P., J.U.D., The Reservation of the Blessed Sacrament, VIII-101 pp., 1927.
41. Doheny, Rev. William J., C.S.C., A.B., J.U.D., Church Property: Modes of Acquisition, X-118 pp., 1927.
42. Feldhaus, Rev. Aloysius H., C.PP.S., J.C.D., Oratories, IX-141 pp., 1927.
43. Kelly, Rev. James Patrick, A.B., J.C.D., The Jurisdiction of the Simple Confessor, X-208 pp., 1927.
44. Neuberger, Rev. Nicholas J., J.C.D., Canon 6 or the Relation of the Codex Juris Canonici to the Preceding Legislation, V-95 pp., 1927.
45. O'Keeffe, Rev. Gerald Michael, J.C.D., Matrimonial Dispensations, Powers of Bishops, Priests, and Confessors, VIII-232 pp., 1927.
46. Quigley, Rev. Joseph, A.M., A.B., J.C.D., Condemned Societies, 139 pp., 1927.
47. Zaplotnik, Rev. Ioannes Leo, J.C.D., De Vicariis Foraneis, X-142 pp., 1927.

48. Duskie, Rev. John Aloysius, A.B., J.C.D., The Canonical Status of the Orientals in the United States, VIII-196 pp., 1928.
49. Hyland, Rev. Francis Edward, J.C.D., Excommunication, Its Nature, Historical Development and Effects, VIII-181 pp., 1928.
50. Reinmann, Rev. Gerald Joseph, O.M.C., J.C.D., The Third Order Secular of Saint Francis, 201 pp., 1928.
51. Schenk, Rev. Francis J., J.C.D., The Matrimonial Impediments of Mixed Religion and Disparity of Cult, XVI-318 pp., 1929.
52. Coady, Rev. John Joseph, S.T.D., J.U.D., A.M., The Appointment of Pastors, VIII-150 pp., 1929.
53. Kay, Rev. Thomas Henry, J.C.D., Competence in Matrimonial Procedure, VIII-164 pp., 1929.
54. Turner, Rev. Sidney Joseph, C.P., J.U.D., The Vow of Poverty, XLIX-217 pp., 1929.
55. Kearney, Rev. Raymond A., A.B., S.T.D., J.C.D., The Principles of Delegation, VII-149 pp., 1929.
56. Conran, Rev. Edward James, A.B., J.C.D., The Interdict, V-163 pp., 1930.
57. O'Neil, Rev. William H., J.C.D., Papal Rescripts of Favor, VII-218 pp.,
58. Bastnagel, Rev. Clement Vincent, J.U.D., The Appointment of Parochial Adjutants and Assistants, XV-257 pp., 1930.
59. Ferry, Rev. William A., A.B., J.C.D., Stole Fees, X-107 pp., 1930.
60. Costello, Rev. John Michael, A.B., J.C.D., Domicile and Quasi-Domicile, VII-201 pp., 1930.
61. Kremer, Rev. Michael Nicholas, A.B., S.T.B., J.C.D., Church Support in the United States, VI-136 pp., 1930.
62. Angulo, Rev. Luis, C.M., J.C.D., Legislación de la Iglesia sobre la intención en la aplicación de la Santa Misa, VII-104 pp., 1931.
63. Frey, Rev. Wolfgang Norbert, O.S.B., A.B., J.C.D., The Act of Religious Profession, VIII-174 pp., 1931.
64. Roberts, Rev. James Brendan, A.B., J.C.D., The Banns of Marriage, XIV-140 pp., 1931.
65. Ryder, Rev. Raymond Aloysius, A.B., J.C.D., Simony, IX-151 pp., 1931.
66. Campagna, Rev. Angelo, Ph.D., J.U.D., Il Vicario Generale del Vescovo, VII-205 pp., 1931.
67. Cox, Rev. Joseph Godfrey, A.B., J.C.D., The Administration of Seminaries, VI-124 pp., 1931.
68. Gregory, Rev. Donald J., J.U.D., The Pauline Privilege, XV-165 pp., 1931.
60. Donohue, Rev. John F., J.C.D., The Impediment of Crime, VIII-110 pp., 1931.
70. Dooley, Rev. Eugene A., O.M.I., J.C.D., Church Law on Sacred Relics, IX-143 pp., 1931.
71. Orth, Rev. Clement Raymond, O.M.C., J.C.D., The Approbation of Religious Institutes, 171 pp., 1931.
72. Pernicone, Rev. Joseph M., A.B., J.C.D., The Ecclesiastical Prohibition of Books, XII-267 pp., 1932.
73. Clinton, Rev. Connell, A.B., J.C.L., The Paschal Precept, 1932.
74. Donnelly, Rev. Francis B., A.M., S.T.L., J.C.L., The Diocesan Synod, 1932

75. Torrente, Rev. Camilo, C.M.F., J.C.L., Las Processiones Sagradas, 1932.
76. Murphy, Rev. Edwin J., C.PP.S., J.C.L., Suspension Ex Informata Conscientia, 1932.
77. MacKenzie, Rev. Eric F., A.M., S.T.L., J.C.L., The Delict of Heresy in its Commission, Penalization, Absolution, 1932.
78. Lyons, Rev. Avitus E., S.T.B., J.C.L., The Collegiate Tribunal of First Instance, 1932.
79. Connolly, Rev. Thomas A., J.C.L., Appeals, 1932.
80. Sangmeister, Rev. Joseph V., A.B., J.C.L., Force and Fear as Precluding Matrimonial Consent, 1932.
81. Jaeger, Rev. Leo A., A.B., J.C.L., The Administration of Vacant and Quasi-Vacant Episcopal Sees in the United States, 1932.
82. Rimlinger, Rev. Herbert T., J.C.L., Error Invalidating Matrimonial Consent, 1932.
83. Barrett, Rev. John D. M., S.S., J.C.L., Comparative Study of the Third Plenary Council and the Code, 1932.

www.ingramcontent.com/pod-product-compliance
Lightning Source LLC
LaVergne TN
LVHW041115090826
844660LV00060B/402

* 9 7 8 0 8 1 3 2 2 2 6 5 3 *